Windows 8 Plain & Simple

Nancy Muir

Published with the authorization of Microsoft Corporation by:
O'Reilly Media, Inc.
1005 Gravenstein Highway North
Sebastopol, California 95472

ISBN: 978-0-7356-6403-6

3 4 5 6 7 8 9 10 11 QG 8 7 6 5 4 3

Printed and bound in the United States of America.

Microsoft Press books are available through booksellers and distributors worldwide. If you need support related to this book, email Microsoft Press Book Support at mspinput@microsoft.com. Please tell us what you think of this book at http://www.microsoft.com/learning/booksurvey.

Microsoft and the trademarks listed at *http://www.microsoft.com/about/legal/en/us/IntellectualProperty/Trademarks/EN-US.aspx* are trademarks of the Microsoft group of companies. All other marks are property of their respective owners.

The example companies, organizations, products, domain names, email addresses, logos, people, places, and events depicted herein are fictitious. No association with any real company, organization, product, domain name, email address, logo, person, place, or event is intended or should be inferred.

This book expresses the author's views and opinions. The information contained in this book is provided without any express, statutory, or implied warranties. Neither the authors, O'Reilly Media, Inc., Microsoft Corporation, nor its resellers, or distributors will be held liable for any damages caused or alleged to be caused either directly or indirectly by this book.

Acquisitions and Developmental Editor: Kenyon Brown
Production Editor: Kristen Borg
Editorial Production: Octal Publishing, Inc.
Interior Composition: Ron Bilodeau
Technical Reviewer: Todd Meister
Indexer: Ron Strauss
Cover Design: Twist Creative • Seattle
Cover Composition: Zyg Group
Illustrator: Rebecca Demarest

[2013-04-26]

To Ebb, for putting up with it all, once again

Contents

1 About This Book 1

2 Meet the Windows 8 Interface 5

What do you think of this book? We want to hear from you!

Microsoft is interested in hearing your feedback so we can continually improve our books and learning resources for you. To participate in a brief online survey, please visit:

www.microsoft.com/learning/booksurvey/

3

Providing Input

21

4

Working with Basic Windows Settings

37

5

Customizing the Appearance of Windows

47

11 Sharing Settings and Files 153

12 Going Online with Internet Explorer 10 163

13

Using Mail and Messaging   171

14

Buying Apps at the Windows Store   185

15

Managing People and Time   193

16 Using the Maps App 213

17 Getting Visual 221

A Upgrading to Windows 8   279

B Keyboard Shortcuts   287

C Getting Help   293

What do you think of this book? We want to hear from you!

Acknowledgments

My sincere thanks to Kenyon Brown for giving me an opportunity to be part of the team of people who worked hard to make this version of this book the best ever. Thanks also to Richard Carey for his able handling of the copyediting aspects of the book, and to Kristen Borg for shepherding the book through the production process while providing a wonderful example of grace under fire. And thanks to the many, many other people who helped to envision, review, produce, and sell this book.

1

About This Book

Knowing how to use your Windows operating system features is key to a successful computing experience. With Windows 8, even those who have used Windows for years will find that they have quite a few new features and interface changes to get used to. This book is designed to give you a simple-to-use visual reference that has you using Windows 8 right away. This book will help you understand the new Windows 8 interface and its touchscreen capabilities, as well as directing you to some more traditional features so that you can use your existing knowledge of Windows to ease your learning curve.

Whether you've used Windows before or are just starting out, this easy-to-understand book takes you through tasks step by step with a friendly visual interface that makes learning intuitive.

A Quick Overview

"Windows 8 Plain & Simple" is divided into sections; each section has a specific focus with related tasks. To help you understand how to move around and use the book, you might want a quick overview of the book's structure.

Section 2, "Meet the Windows 8 Interface," and Section 3, "Providing Input," provide an introduction to the Windows 8 interface and the basic skills you need to navigate its features. You discover how to start and shut down Windows, get help, and how to provide input with your mouse, keyboard, or fingers by using a touchscreen.

Section 4, "Working with Basic Windows Settings," covers commonly used Windows settings, such as setting the date and time, connecting to an available network, and adjusting screen brightness. Section 5, "Customizing the Appearance of Windows," leads you through common tasks associated with personalizing your computer by modifying settings for colors, backgrounds, and more. You learn how to organize and customize tiles on the Start screen, as well.

Section 6, "Working with Users and Privacy," shows you how to work with user accounts and security tools such as Family Safety, Windows Firewall, and Windows Defender. Section 7, "Working with Accessibility Settings," helps you understand how the Ease Of Access settings can make using your computer easier if you have vision, hearing, or dexterity challenges.

Section 8, "Searching," covers all the tools Windows 8 offers for searching content both on your computer and online. In Section 9, "Working with Apps," you learn about using applications, such as finding and opening an app, zooming in and out, and entering text. You also discover the ins and outs of saving and printing files. Section 10, "File Management," offers valuable steps for managing those files in Windows folders and libraries.

Section 11, "Sharing Settings and Files," and Section 12, "Going Online with Internet Explorer 10," get you online, connecting to the Internet and learning to use the new features of the Internet Explorer 10 browser to navigate the web. You also discover how to sync your computer settings and content so that you can access them from anywhere.

Section 13, "Using Mail and Messaging," covers how to use an email account and the pre-installed Messaging app. In Section 14, "Buying Apps at the Windows Store," you learn how to shop at the Windows Store for apps and more.

Section 15, "Managing People and Time," provides steps for managing your contacts and time by using the People, Calendar, and Weather apps. Section 16, "Using the Maps App," introduces you to the useful Maps app to help you find your way. Section 17, "Getting Visual" and Section 18, "Playing Music" are all about having fun playing music and videos, and even taking your own videos and photos.

Section 19, "Working with Devices and Networks," and Section 20, "Maintaining and Troubleshooting Your Computer," provide the practical content that helps you connect with a network, manage your security and privacy, and maintain Windows to keep it trouble-free.

Finally, Appendix A, "Upgrading to Windows 8," provides a comparison of Windows 8 features with earlier versions of Windows that might help you in your transition to the newer operating system; Appendix B, "Keyboard Shortcuts," gives you a handy list of keystroke shortcuts; and Appendix C, "Getting Help," offers suggestions about how to get more help.

A Few Assumptions

In writing any book, it's important to make a few assumptions about your readers. I assume that you are basically computer literate, meaning that you have used a computer before and know how to turn it on and turn it off, how to use a mouse, and how to select text and objects such as drawn shapes or photos. I also assume that you have worked with some kind of software before and know what a menu, dialog box, and tool button are. I do not assume that you have used a touchscreen before because this is a relatively recent addition to computers.

I assume that you use computers either at work or at home, or both, and that you have access to an Internet connection and have experience using one browser or another. Other than that, I try to give you all the steps you need to get things done in an easy-to-understand way, no matter what your technical background.

What's New in Windows 8?

The biggest changes in Windows 8 involve the way things appear in the Windows Start screen, as well as the ability to interact with Windows by using a touchscreen.

Windows 8 makes excellent use of online resources and third-party apps, somewhat akin to the way the average smartphone does. With an Internet connection, you'll find that on-screen elements update you in real time about everything from stocks and weather to activity on your social networking sites. Because you're probably connected with many people in a variety of ways, Windows 8 gives you the ability to share content with others easily. Also, Windows Live ID and Windows To Go features allow you to access your content from wherever you are.

If you've used File Explorer before, you'll find that it now includes a ribbon, with tools similar to those you might have used in a recent version of Microsoft Office.

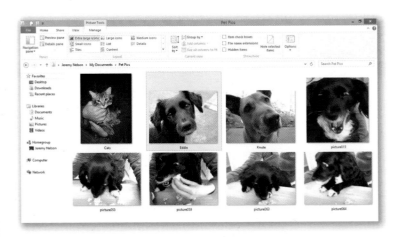

The Final Word

Your computer has become vital to your productivity and entertainment, so why shouldn't your computing experience be pleasant and fun? In this book, I try to offer short tasks to get you working with Windows 8 quickly and painlessly. I keep the technical terminology and explanations to a minimum, all within a visually appealing book that immediately connects you to what you see on screen. My goal is to get you less focused on the tool and more focused on what you can do with it to make your life simpler.

I hope you find the structure and design of this book easy to navigate and helpful as you get up to speed with all the wonderful new features in Windows 8.

Meet the Windows 8 Interface

The big news for Windows 8 is all about the interface. The main interface is the Start screen, a brand-new look and approach. The Start screen is simple and clean in appearance. Rather than having a Start menu from which you open programs and settings, you have a set of tiles on the screen. Click a tile, and an application (now called an app) opens.

To find apps not represented by tiles on the Start screen, use a great new search feature; simply start typing the name of an app, file, or setting on the Start screen, and a master index of content appears.

To keep the Start screen uncluttered, several useful tools called charms are hidden until you reveal them. Use charms to review common settings, share content, search, and more.

In addition to the Start screen, there is the Windows 8 desktop. This more closely resembles the traditional Windows desktop, minus a Start menu. The desktop provides shortcuts to files and apps as well as a taskbar displaying frequently used programs and settings. You can also access charms from the desktop, and several handy keystroke shortcuts let you move back and forth from the Start screen to desktop.

In this section, you become familiar with both sides of the Windows 8 interface.

Starting Windows 8

When you first turn on your computer or when your computer has fallen asleep after an interval of inactivity, you will see the lock screen. The lock screen displays a pretty picture as well as some information such as time and weather. (See Section 5 for how to change this picture and the information displayed on the screen.) At this point, you need to hide the lock screen, choose a user account with which to log on, and enter a password or PIN to get to the Start screen.

Start Your Computer and Log On to Windows 8

1. Press the power button to start your computer.

2. Drag the bottom of the lock screen up.

3 Click the Switch User arrow to the left of the currently displayed account picture.

4 Click a user to log on as.

5 Enter your password or PIN.

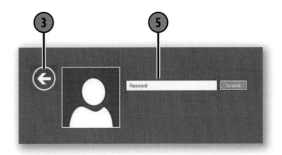

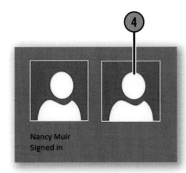

Tip

The lock screen appears after a certain interval of inactivity or if you choose Sleep from the power settings by using the Settings charm. To quickly go to the lock screen at any time, you can use the keystroke combination Windows logo key+L.

Switching from a Local to a Microsoft Live Account

You can log on to your computer by using local settings (with no settings coming from the Internet), or you can log on by using a Microsoft Live account. When you use a Live account, which requires that you get a free email account from Microsoft, you enable every Windows device you use to sync settings from your computer and access your documents from anywhere. See Section 11, "Sharing Settings and Files," for more about these features.

Set Up to Log On by Using Microsoft Live

1. Press Windows logo key+I.
2. Click Change PC Settings.
3. Click Users.
4. Click Switch To A Microsoft Account.
5. Enter your email address.
6. Click Next.
7. Enter your password and click Next.
8. Review your contact information and then click Next.
9. Click Finish.

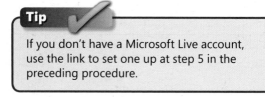

Tip

If you don't have a Microsoft Live account, use the link to set one up at step 5 in the preceding procedure.

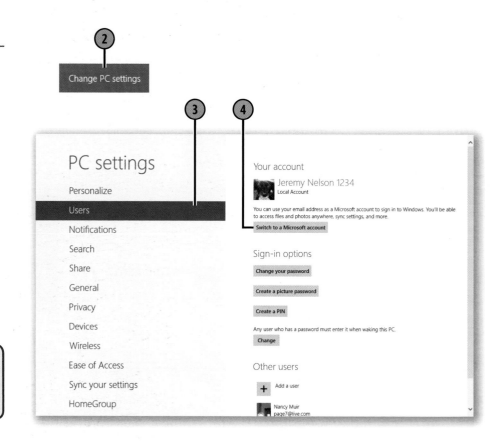

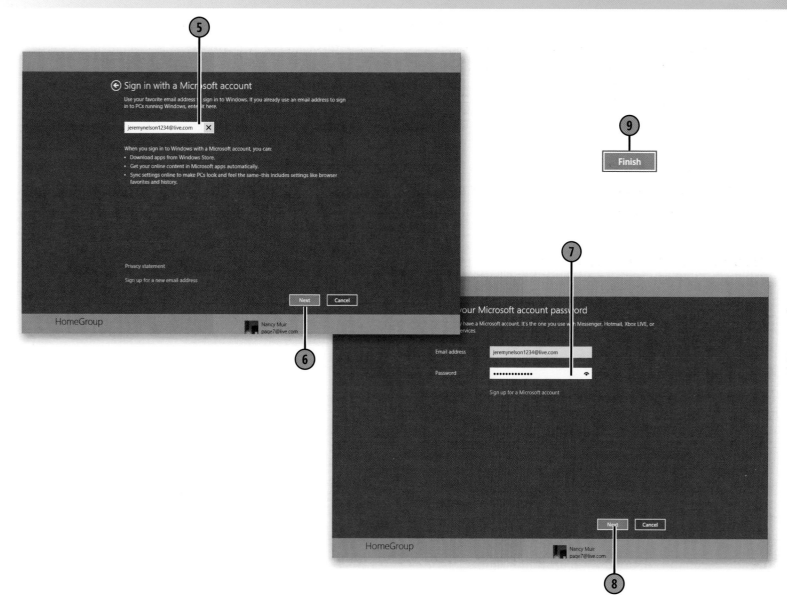

Exploring the Start Screen and Desktop

Moving between the Start screen and desktop is easy, and you'll find you need to do this for a few reasons. First, there are some settings that are available from the Control Panel that aren't available in the PC Settings dialog that you access from the Settings charm. In addition, the version of Internet Explorer that you access from the desktop is different from the version you access from the Start screen.

Switch Between Start Screen and the Desktop

① Press the Windows logo key.

② Click the Desktop tile.

③ Press Windows logo key+C.

④ Click the Start button.

Tip

You don't have to go to the desktop to open the Control Panel. You can simply begin typing **Control Panel** from the Start screen and then click the Control Panel app in the search results that appear.

Overview of the Start Screen

The Start screen is a simple, clean interface that puts the focus on tiles, but there are a few other things going on, such as a scroll bar along the bottom so that you can use to scroll among tiles; an account settings button in the upper-right corner for changing users or account pictures; and charms that you can display whenever you need them.

Tiles   Account Settings

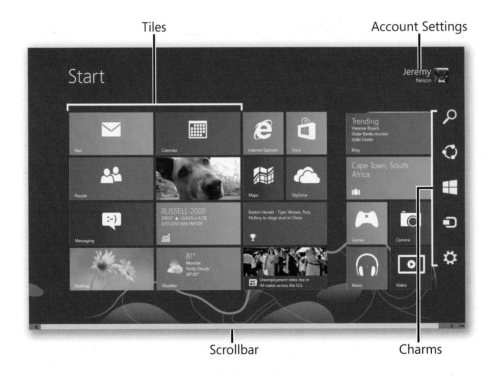

Scrollbar   Charms

Understanding Tiles

Tiles make frequently used apps and settings available in a graphical way rather than presenting these options in a menu. If you own a touchscreen device, they're even more convenient because you can simply tap a tile to open an app. So-called "live" tiles offer up-to-the-minute information for certain apps if you are logged on with a Microsoft Live account. You can easily add, remove, or rearrange tiles on the Start screen. (See Section 5 for more about personalizing the Start screen.)

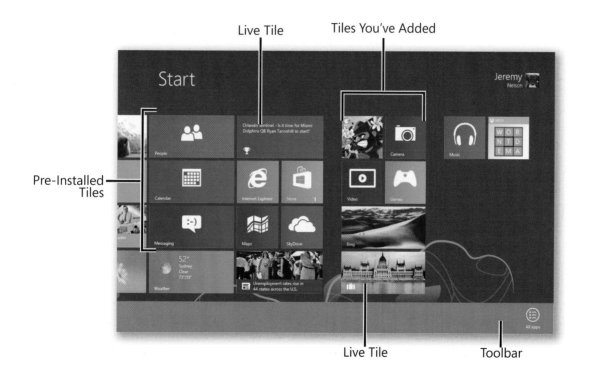

Live Tile

Tiles You've Added

Pre-Installed Tiles

Live Tile

Toolbar

Using Charms

Charms allow you to access features such as Search and sharing, as well as settings for devices and various PC features. There is also a charm that you can click to return to the Start screen from anywhere. When you click the Settings charm, you are taken to a subpanel on which you can access six commonly used settings, such as Volume, or to display the PC Settings panel to access a more complete menu of settings.

Display and Use Charms

1. Press Windows logo key+C to display the charms.
2. Click Search.
3. Click an app to open it.
4. Press Windows logo key+I to display the settings subpanel of the charms.
5. Click the Volume button.
6. Drag the Volume Slider up.
7. Click outside of the list of charms to hide them.

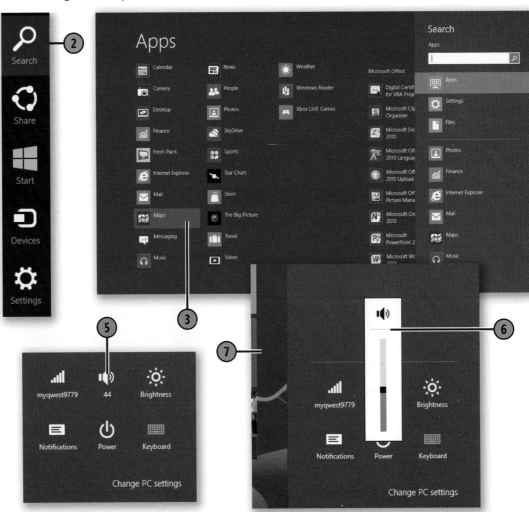

Overview of the Desktop

The desktop in Windows 8 has many features you will be familiar with if you've used previous versions of Windows, such as the desktop background, desktop shortcuts, and the taskbar.

The desktop is useful for accessing the Control Panel from the Settings charm; opening File Explorer from the Quick Access Bar; and changing common settings such as the volume or date and time from icons on the Taskbar.

Desktop Shortcuts

Quick Access Bar   Taskbar

Working with Apps in Windows

When you open apps from the desktop, they open in the familiar format of windows. You can move these windows around your screen, and you can minimize, maximize, and resize them.

You can even snap windows to the side of the screen so that you can easily display more than one at a time.

Navigate Within and Among Windows

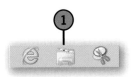

① Click File Explorer in the desktop taskbar.

② Click the title bar of the window, and quickly drag it to the left to "snap" it to the left side of the screen.

③ Click the title bar and drag the window away from the edge of the screen.

④ Click a corner and drag inward to reduce the size of the window.

⑤ Click to maximize the window.

⑥ Click to restore the window to its smaller size.

⑦ Click Internet Explorer.

⑧ Press Alt+Tab to move among the open windows.

⑨ Click the Close button in the upper-right corner to close the windows.

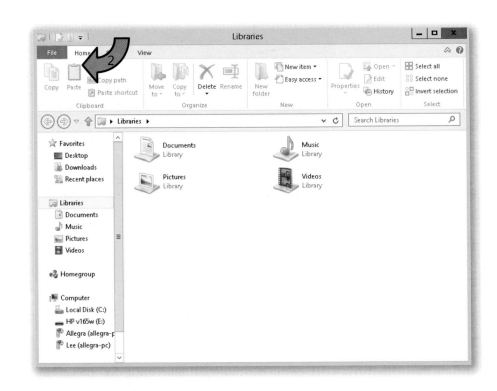

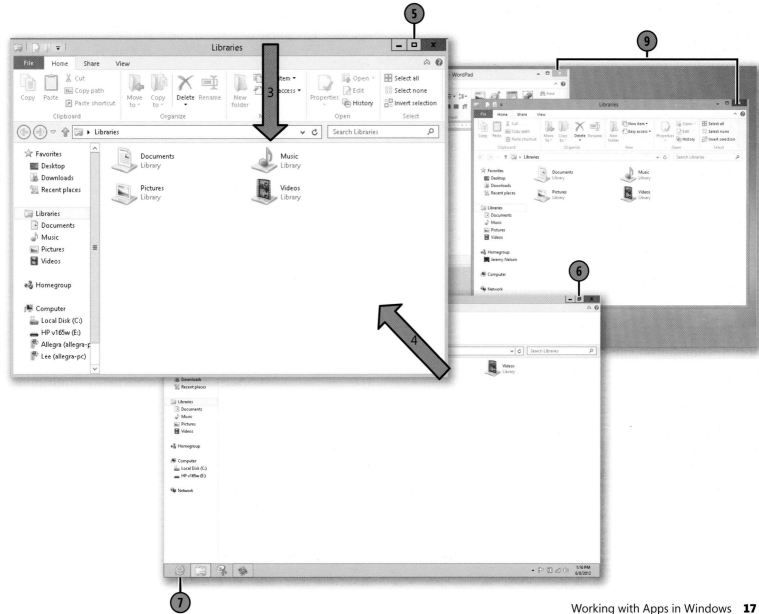

Adding Shortcuts to the Desktop

Think of desktop shortcuts as the precursors to tiles on the Start screen. They give you quick access to individual apps or files, and with the loss of the Start menu in Windows 8, they are the only way to get to these items from the desktop aside from browsing for them by using File Explorer. Creating shortcuts is simple.

Create Shortcuts on the Desktop

1. Click File Explorer.
2. Locate a file, folder, or app.
3. Right click.
4. Choose Send To, Desktop (Create Shortcut).

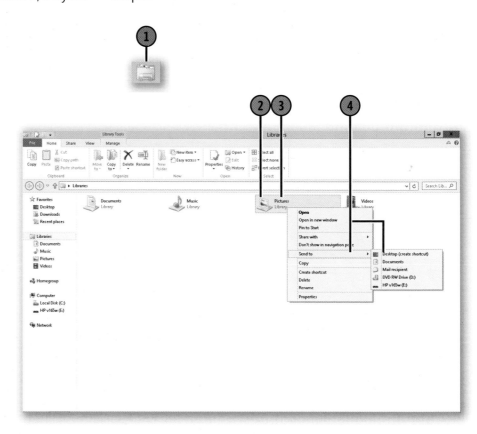

> ### Tip
>
> If you find you don't need a shortcut any-more, just right-click it on the desktop and choose Delete. If you'd like to pin the item from a shortcut to the Start screen, right-click the shortcut and choose Pin To Start. To place a shortcut on the desktop taskbar, choose Pin To Taskbar from the same menu.

Working with the Taskbar

The desktop taskbar is an area at the bottom of the screen that contains buttons you can click to quickly start frequently used apps as well as buttons for actions you take often, such as displaying the onscreen keyboard, connecting to a network, or adjusting the system volume. If you're familiar with earlier versions of Windows, you will recognize most of the functions of the taskbar.

Find Out What You Can Do with the Taskbar

1. Click File Explorer on the Quick Launch portion of the taskbar.

2. On the right side of the taskbar, click the Volume setting.

3. Right-click the taskbar.

4. Click Properties.

5. Click Lock The Taskbar to always keep the taskbar on your screen.

6. Click Taskbar Location On Screen.

7. Choose a different location.

8. Click Apply.

9. Click Taskbar Location On Screen.

10. Choose Bottom.

11. Click OK.

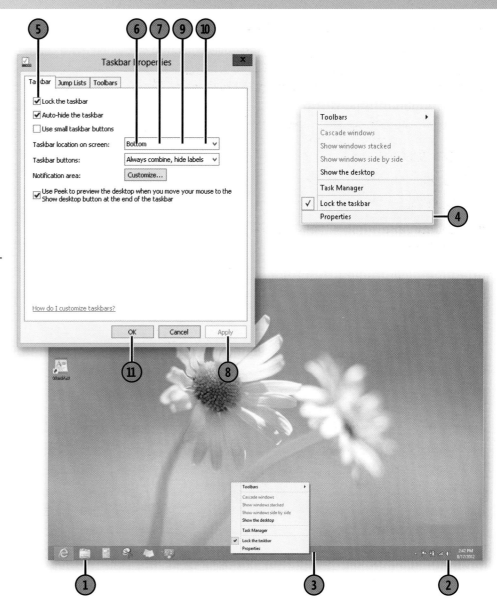

Overview of File Explorer

File Explorer will be familiar to users of earlier versions of Windows. This feature gives you access to all the drives of your computer, from your hard drive to DVD, external, and USB drives. File Explorer is also the best way to browse the contents of your computer, including libraries, folders, and individual files. To access File Explorer, simply press Windows logo key+E. (See Section 10, "File Management," for more about using File Explorer.)

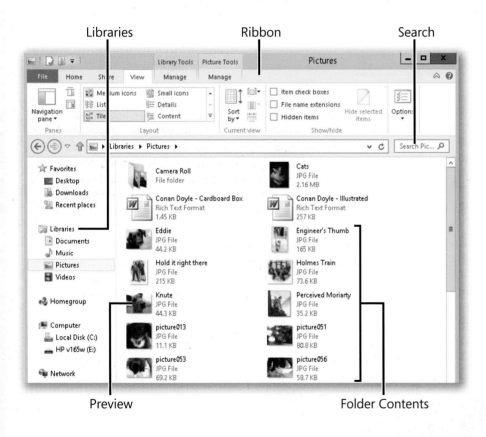

Libraries   Ribbon   Search

Preview   Folder Contents

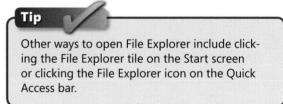

Tip

Other ways to open File Explorer include clicking the File Explorer tile on the Start screen or clicking the File Explorer icon on the Quick Access bar.

3

Providing Input

Just as you can use a pen to put words on paper, you need some method for inputting data into a computer. Traditionally, computer users have used a mouse and a keyboard to provide input. For example, you might use a mouse to select and move an object or text or to display a menu of commands and select one. You use your keyboard to enter text in a memo or spreadsheet or to implement a command, such as deleting selected text with the Delete key.

In Windows 8, one very interesting input method has been added: your own fingers. If you have a touchscreen computer or computing device such as a tablet, you can use a finger or a stylus to input onscreen gestures and to type on an onscreen keyboard.

This section provides information about the three input methods and how to use them to control various interactions with your computer. Because touchscreen computers are still relatively rare, the rest of this book assumes the use of the mouse and keyboard methods of input.

Understanding Input Options

Touchscreen devices have arrived in the form of tablet computers such as iPad and Kindle Fire, and touchscreen computer models are a growing trend. Windows 8 has therefore been designed to take advantage of this input method. However, because many people are more comfortable with traditional input methods, Windows 8 also lets you use a mouse and keyboard to accomplish any task. In the following task, you can compare three methods of initiating the Search feature.

Perform Actions One of Three Ways

1️⃣ Right-click the Start screen.

2️⃣ Click the All Apps button.

3️⃣ Press the Windows logo key to return to the Start screen.

4️⃣ Press Windows logo key+Q.

5️⃣ Press the Windows logo key to return to the Start screen.

6️⃣ Using your finger, swipe from the right side of the screen inward.

7️⃣ Tap the Search charm.

Overview of Touchscreen Gestures

With a touchscreen device, you use your finger to tap buttons or objects, swipe across the screen to display toolbars, swipe up and down in a document or on a webpage to move through the content, and more. Here's an overview of touch gestures to get you started.

Use Touch to Get Things Done

1. With the Start screen displayed, tap a tile.

2. Swipe from the right side of the screen inward.

3. Tap the Start charm to return to the Start screen.

4. Tap another tile.

5. Swipe from the top of the screen downward to close the app and go back to the Start screen.

6. Swipe from right to left across the Start screen to display more tiles.

7. Tap the Internet Explorer tile.

8. Swipe your finger up and down the page to scroll through its content.

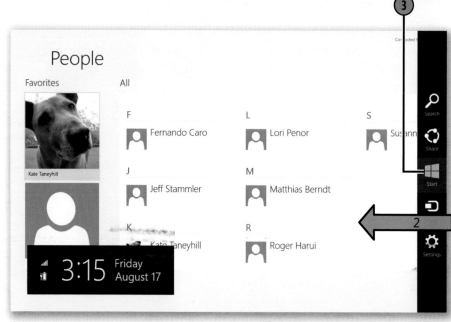

Swiping Corners and Edges

In Windows 8, you can use the corners and edges of the screen to take three important actions. You can display charms, which give you access to various settings and the Start screen; you can display recently used and open apps to move among apps; finally, you can swipe down from the top of the screen to close an app.

Swipe the Screen

1. Tap an app tile on the Start screen.
2. Swipe down to close the app.
3. Swipe from the right to display charms.
4. Swipe up to display a toolbar.

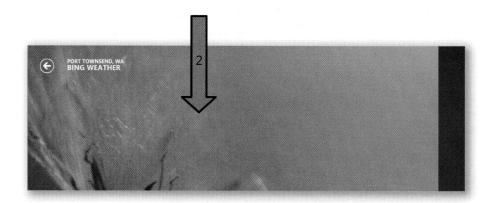

Tip

You can use your mouse to click tiles and to drag an app downward to close it. To display charms, you simply move your mouse to the upper-right or lower-right corner without clicking. In many apps, you can display toolbars by simply right-clicking.

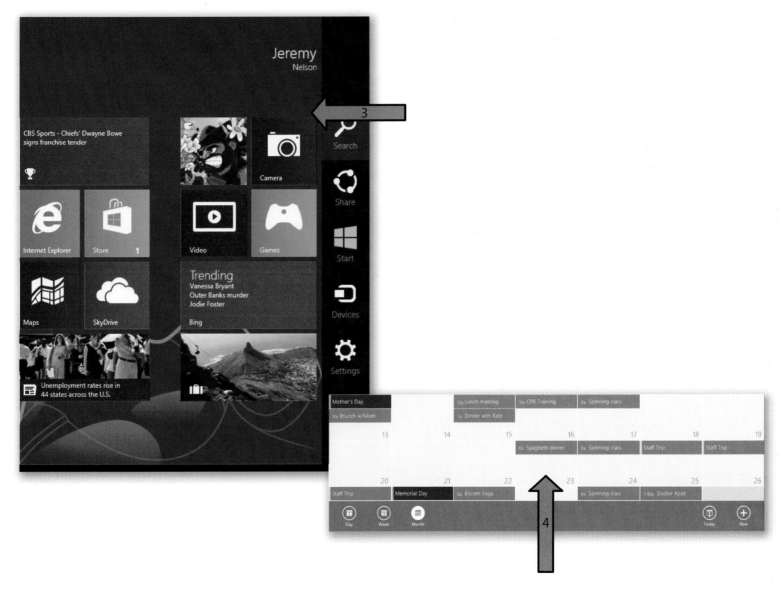

Enlarging or Reducing the Display

You can use your fingers to reduce the size of the current display in certain apps, such as on a webpage in Internet Explorer or in a document in Microsoft Word. You can also use a new feature called *Semantic Zoom* to reduce the tiles on the Start screen. This is useful if you have pinned several apps to the Start screen and want to get an overview of all the apps you have available.

Enlarge or Reduce the Display

1. With the Start screen displayed, press your thumb and forefinger apart on the screen and swipe them toward one another.

2. Press your thumb and forefinger together on the screen, and swipe them away from one another.

3. Tap the Internet Explorer tile.

4. Press your thumb and forefinger together on the screen, and swipe them away from one another.

5. Press your thumb and forefinger apart on the screen, and swipe them toward one another.

Tip

The action of moving your fingers apart or together on a touchscreen is often referred to as unpinching and pinching.

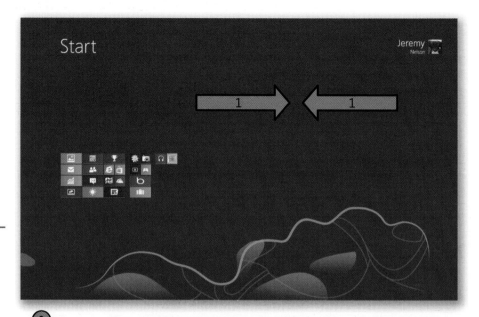

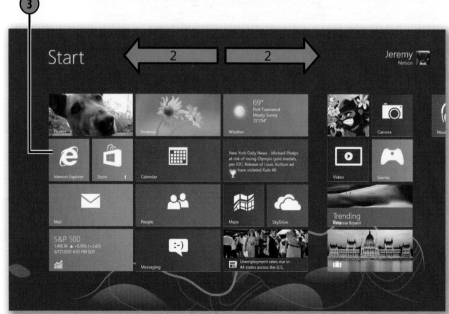

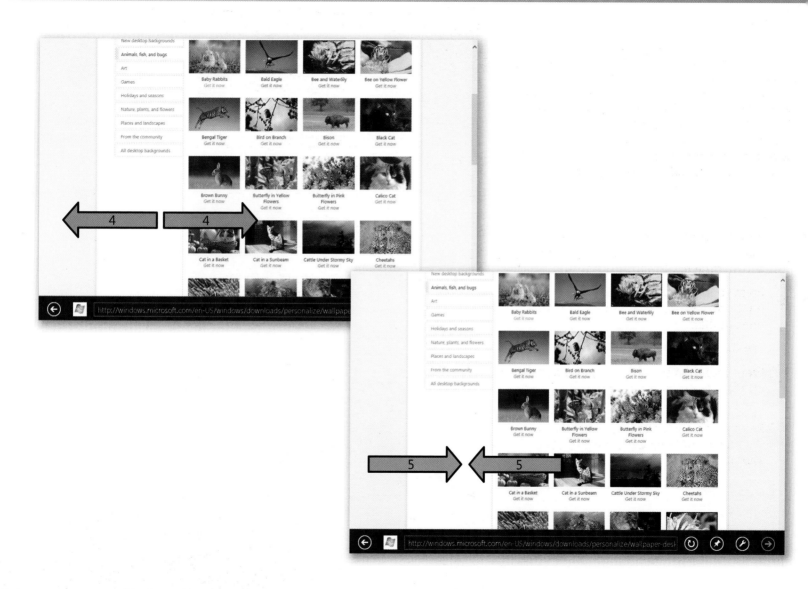

Snapping Apps

The ability to snap apps isn't new with Windows 8, but the ability to snap by using a touchscreen adds an interesting dimension. Snapping helps you to organize more than one app on your screen to view their contents side by side. You can also snap an app to display it full screen with a single swipe of your finger or drag of your mouse on an app's title bar. This action takes a bit of getting used to, and, of course, it requires that you have a touchscreen, so if you do, you can get some practice here.

Snap an App

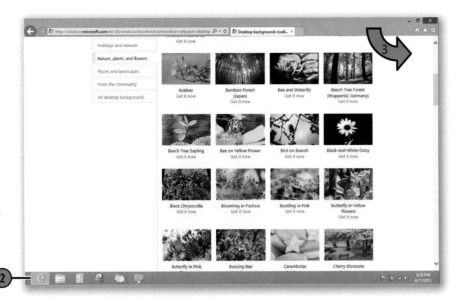

1. On the Start screen, tap the Desktop tile.

2. Tap the Internet Explorer shortcut on the taskbar.

3. Press your finger on the Internet Explorer title bar (the top of the window), and "snap" it to the right edge of the screen.

4. Tap the File Explorer shortcut on the taskbar.

5. Press your finger on the File Explorer title bar, and snap it to the left edge of the screen.

6. Press your finger on the Internet Explorer title bar, and snap it to the top edge of the screen.

> **Tip**
>
> To snap using a mouse, simply click an app's title bar and drag it to the right, left, or up. Left or right changes a reduced window to full screen and changes a full screen to half screen. Dragging up displays an app full screen. You can also press the Windows logo key along with the Right key or Left key to snap an open window.

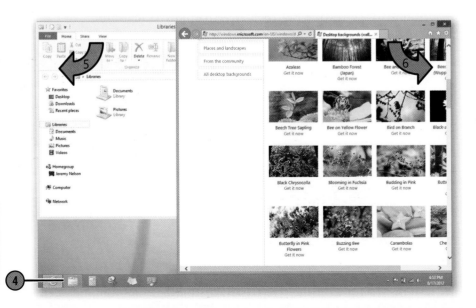

Using a Touchscreen Keyboard

You might need to get used to the way an onscreen keyboard works if you've never used one. The biggest difference with the default settings for the onscreen keyboard is that you have to change to an alternate keyboard to access numbers and most punctuation; on a physical keyboard, these items occupy a row near the top of the keyboard. You should also know how to display and hide the onscreen keyboard.

Use the Touch Keyboard

(1) From the Start screen, begin typing **WordPad**.

(2) Tap the WordPad app in the search results.

(3) Tap the Keyboard button.

(4) Tap keys to enter a word.

(5) Tap the Symbol/Number key.

(6) Tap keys to enter punctuation or numbers.

(7) Tap the Symbol/Number key again to display the letter keyboard.

(8) Tap the Expand/Shrink button to expand the keyboard.

(9) Tap the Close key to hide the keyboard.

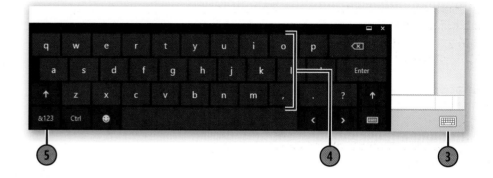

Displaying Charms

Charms are buttons for accessing common device settings. For example, there is a charm that displays the Start screen, as well as one that displays the Search feature. You can use these settings to change system volume, put your device to sleep or turn it off, and connect to a network. You can display the charms by using your mouse, keyboard, or touchscreen.

Display Charms

You can display the charms by using any of the following three techniques.

1. Swipe your finger inward from the right edge of the screen.

2. Press Windows logo key+C on your keyboard.

3. Move your mouse to the upper-right or lower-right corner of the screen.

Tip

You can display the charms from both the desktop and the Start screen by using any of these methods.

Using Keystroke Shortcuts

Your keyboard also provides a great way to get things done with keystroke shortcuts. This involves pressing one key and then, while holding down that key, pressing another key or two.

By using these special keystroke combinations, you can access the Search feature, move from one open app to another, display the charms, and much more.

Examples of Keystroke Shortcuts

1. Press the Windows logo key to display the Start screen.

2. Press Windows logo key+C to display the charms.

3. Press Windows logo key+Q to display the Search feature for apps.

4. Press Windows logo key+R to go to the desktop, and enter a program or file name to run.

5. Press the Windows logo key to return to the Start screen.

6. Press Windows logo key+Tab to display recently used apps.

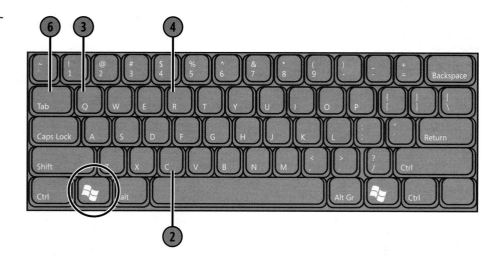

Tip

See Appendix B, "Keyboard Shortcuts," for a more complete listing of useful keystroke shortcuts.

Right-Clicking to Display Tools

Right-clicking has traditionally been a way to display command menus that are contextually relevant to where you click. For example, if you right-click selected text in a Word document, you can see commands such as Cut and Copy. In Windows 8, right-clicking can also display tools on the Start screen to help you find apps or apply settings to individual app tiles. When you access Internet Explorer 10 from the Start screen, right-clicking is one way to display the Address bar.

Use Right-Click

1. From the Start screen, right-click a tile to display a set of tools.

2. Right-click the tile again to deselect it.

3. Right-click the Start screen background.

4. Click the All Apps button to display the Search feature.

5. Click Internet Explorer in the search results.

6. Right-click the page to display the address bar.

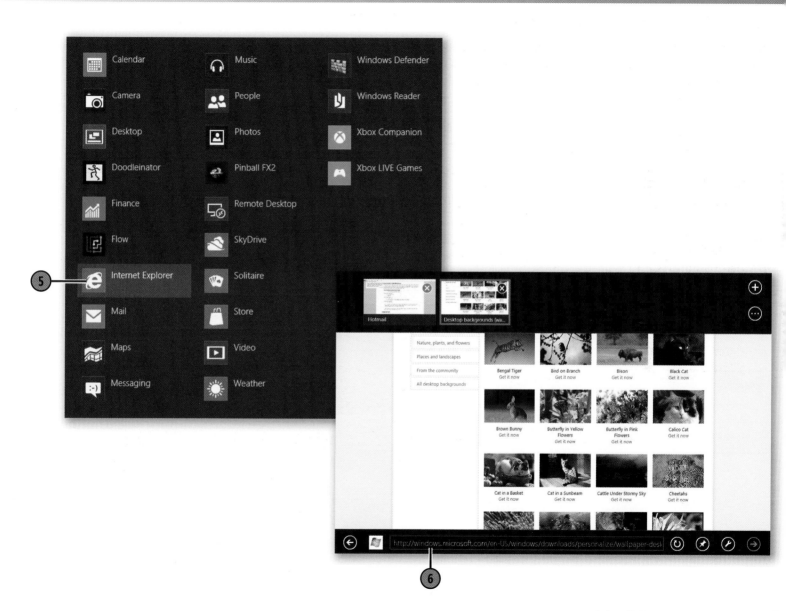

Finding Recently Viewed Apps

In Windows 8, you don't really close apps from the Start screen. You open apps and then return to the Start screen or search for another app or file to open. You can display all open apps and jump back to one by using a new feature. By moving your mouse to the upper-left edge of the screen, you can go to any recently opened app quickly.

View and Open Recent Apps

1. From either the desktop or Start screen, move your mouse to the upper-left corner of the screen.

2. Slide your mouse down the left edge of the screen.

3. Click a thumbnail to go to a recently viewed app.

Tip

Currently open apps are displayed on the taskbar in the desktop. Simply click one to maximize an app.

Working with Basic Windows Settings

4

Windows 8 settings provide tools for managing your Windows experience. You can access these settings in two ways: through the Settings charm or through the Control Panel. The Settings charm offers access to the most commonly used settings. If you want to dig deeper into more advanced settings, you will probably use the Control Panel.

Some basic settings, such as choosing what network to connect to or changing the date and time for your computer clock and calendars, are used at one time or another by most people. In this section, you'll learn how to modify some of the most commonly used Windows 8 settings. When you click the Settings charm, common PC settings are displayed, along with a Change PC Settings link to access more settings.

Displaying Windows Settings

Windows has included the Control Panel feature for many years. While the Control Panel is still available in Windows 8, the most commonly used settings for Windows can now be reached by using the charms, which you can display along the right edge of either the Start screen or the desktop. Tapping the Settings charm displays a group of commonly used settings.

Display Common Settings

(1) Press the Windows logo key+C to display the charms.

(2) Click the Settings charm.

(3) Click any setting in the bottom of the panel to access its controls.

Charm	Results
Volume	Displays a slider to adjust system volume
Brightness	Displays a slider to adjust screen brightness
Network	Displays a list of available networks
Notifications	Offers settings for hiding notifications
Power	Displays three commands offering sleep, shut down, or restart options
Keyboard	Offers settings for language and displaying keyboard

See Also

See "Overview of Touchscreen Gestures" on page 24 to learn the gesture you can use to display the charms on a touch-screen computing device.

Connecting to a Network

Especially when you're on the go, you will need to connect to and disconnect from different networks and hotspots (publicly available networks in places like airports and coffee shops). You can quickly perform these actions by using the Network button accessed by clicking the Settings charm. Windows 8 will automatically search for and display available networks for you to connect to, and you simply choose the one you want to use.

Connect or Disconnect from a Network

1. Press Windows logo key+C.
2. Click Settings.
3. Click the Network button.
4. Click a network connection.
5. If you aren't connected, click the Connect button.
6. To disconnect, click the Disconnect button.

Controlling Volume

Some individual desktop apps, such as Music, have their own volume controls. However, the Windows system volume is a master control. For example, if you set the system volume to 50 percent, app volume controls can't make the volume any louder than that. Setting an app volume to 80 percent would mean that it's playing at 80 percent of the Windows system volume setting. It's quite common to want to adjust the system volume or mute sound entirely, which you can do using the Volume slider.

Adjust System Volume

1. Press Windows logo key+C.
2. Click Settings.
3. Click the Volume button.
4. Click and drag the slider to raise or lower volume.

If you want to get separate control over the volume of your system and the volume of system sounds, such as an alert that an email has arrived, display the Control Panel (type "Control Panel" from the Start Screen, and click the app in the search results), click Hardware And Sound, and then click Sound, Adjust System Volume. Click and drag the System Sounds slider up or down to adjust it.

You can mute sound on your computer by dragging the slider to the very bottom of the Volume setting.

Adjusting Brightness

The brightness setting for your screen is most important on laptops and tablets, which are typically less crisp than larger desktop displays. Also, because these devices might be used in different lighting conditions as you travel from place to place, you'll find yourself adjusting their brightness more often. Adjusting brightness is easy, using a simple slider setting.

Set Brightness

1. Press Windows logo key+C.
2. Click Settings.
3. Click the Brightness button.
4. Click and drag the slider to increase or decrease brightness.

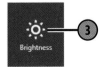

Changing the Time and Date

Your computer uses the time zone you specify in Windows to display clocks on the Windows Desktop taskbar, set calendar applications to the correct date, run scheduled maintenance tasks, and so on. The time zone you select automatically sets the correct date and time, even taking into account areas that don't use daylight savings time. If your location doesn't use daylight savings time, you can use a setting to turn off automatic adjustments.

You probably set up your time zone when you first set up Windows 8. However, today's computers often don't stay on the desktop: laptops go on the road with business people and vacationers, desktop computers go to different time zones when the family moves across the country, and so on. It's handy to know how to change the time zone.

Change the Time Zone

1. Press Windows logo key+C.

2. Click Settings.

3. Click the Change PC Settings link.

4. Click General.

5. Click the Time Zone field to display a list of options.

6. Click an option to select it.

Tip

You can use settings on the Control Panel to manually set the time and date rather than having them automatically set based on your time zone. If you're traveling and not sure what time zone you're in, but you happen to know the time and date, the manual option could be useful.

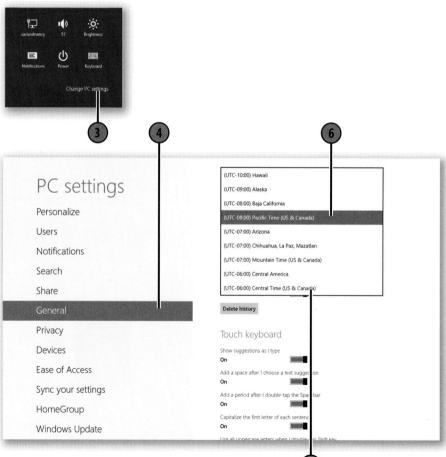

Adjust for Daylight Savings Time

① With the PC Settings screen displayed, tap General.

② Click the Adjust Clock for Daylight Saving Time Automatically slider.

Tip

Windows allows you to add clocks for different time zones when you want to know the time in other locations, such as a branch office or plant. Look for the Add Clocks For Different Time Zones setting in the Clock, Language, And Region area of the Control Panel.

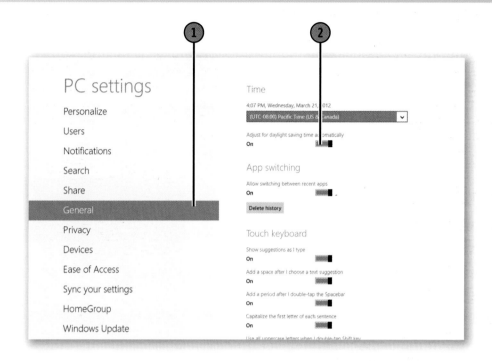

PC settings

Personalize
Users
Notifications
Search
Share
General
Privacy
Devices
Ease of Access
Sync your settings
HomeGroup
Windows Update

Time

4:07 PM, Wednesday, March 21, 2012

(UTC-08:00) Pacific Time (US & Canada)

Adjust for daylight saving time automatically
On

App switching

Allow switching between recent apps
On

Delete history

Touch keyboard

Show suggestions as I type
On

Add a space after I choose a text suggestion
On

Add a period after I double-tap the Spacebar
On

Capitalize the first letter of each sentence
On

Use all uppercase letters when I double-tap Shift key

Managing Power

Windows allows you to put your computer to sleep, which saves battery power if you have a laptop or tablet, and displays a black screen useful for hiding your work from others. You can also restart your computer, which you'll need to do when you install or run certain apps to put changes into effect. Restarting can also sometimes solve problems you're experiencing. Finally, if you won't be using your computer for a while, you can shut it down, again saving battery power for portable devices or electricity for a wired computer.

Put to Sleep, Shut Down, or Restart Your Computer

① Press Windows logo key+C.

② Click Settings.

③ Click the Power button.

④ Click the Sleep, Shut Down, or Restart command, depending on what you want to do.

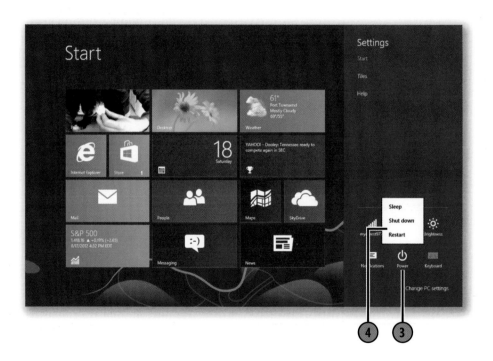

Displaying the Keyboard

If you like the onscreen keyboard or have to use this feature because you're using a tablet Windows 8 device with no physical keyboard, you'll appreciate the Keyboard settings. In the Settings charm panel you can click Keyboard to view the currently selected language for the keyboard and display the keyboard and handwriting panel. The handwriting panel allows you to enter text by "writing" with your mouse or finger if you have a touchscreen computer.

Display the Keyboard and Handwriting Panel

① Press Windows logo key+C.

② Click Settings.

③ Click Keyboard.

④ Click Touch Keyboard And Handwriting Panel.

⑤ Click to choose the keyboard format.

⑥ Click Handwriting Panel.

⑦ Click and draw a word or shape on the screen.

Tip

Use the keyboard format setting to display a split screen. This style of screen makes it easier to type on a smaller device such as a Windows 8 tablet, where you might use both your thumbs to hit keys on different edges of the screen.

Customizing the Appearance of Windows

The ability to adjust the appearance of Windows (known as the interface) lets you set up your computer to look the way you want it and lets you organize the tools and apps you use often so that you can find them easily.

You can customize the Start screen by controlling what apps appear there and the size of each app tile, as well as modifying the screen's background pattern and its color. You can also personalize the Lock screen by setting up a new background image. You can modify Lock screen notifications, which are apps that display information even when your screen is locked.

Finally, as in previous versions of Windows, you can use the Control Panel to make changes to the desktop's appearance, including its background, color scheme, and your display's screen resolution.

Customizing the Start Screen

The Start screen is your new home screen in Windows 8. It is similar to the Windows Mobile operating system interface used in some smartphones and tablets. The Start screen contains tiles that represent installed apps such as File Explorer and Maps. You can customize the Start screen by pinning and unpinning apps so that those that you use most often appear there. You can also adjust the size of some tiles to be smaller or larger. For example, you might make the tile for an app that you use all the time larger so that you can spot it easily, or make several tiles smaller so that Windows can fit more apps on the screen.

Pin an App

1. On the Start screen, press Windows logo key+Q to display a list of apps.

2. Right-click an app.

3. Click Pin To Start.

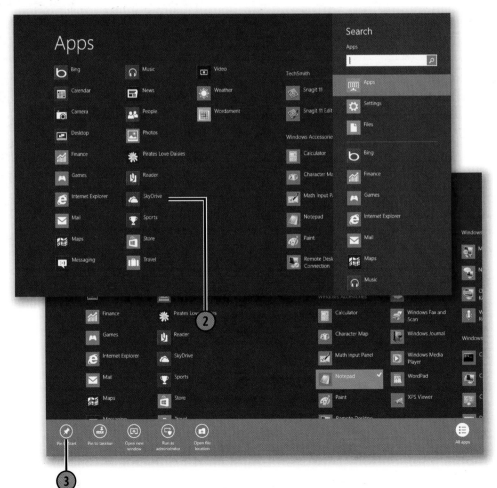

Unpin an App

1 Display the Start screen.

2 Right-click a pinned app.

3 Click Unpin from Start.

Tip

You can pin an active item to the desktop taskbar by right-clicking it and choosing Pin This Program To Taskbar. Then, if you want to unpin the app, just right-click it in the taskbar, and in the menu that appears, choose Unpin This Program From Taskbar.

Modifying Tiles on the Start Screen

You might have noticed that tiles on the Start screen come in different sizes. Some are larger, such as Weather; others are smaller. Certain tiles can be made smaller or larger. These include the Desktop, Xbox LIVE Games, Weather, Music, Photo, and Messaging tiles. Being able to adjust the size of some tiles helps you fit the items you want to access on the Start screen in an organized way.

Change Tile Size

1. Right-click a tile. (Not all tiles will offer this option, so test this with the Calendar or Weather app.)

2. Click Smaller. (If the tile is already smaller, click Larger.)

Tip

If you like to keep a lot of tiles on the Start screen, consider reducing the size of those that offer that option so that you don't have to scroll as much to find what you need.

Move Tiles in Start Screen

① Display the Start screen.

② Click a tile, and drag it to a new location.

③ Release your mouse button.

Try This!

After you have installed a few apps of your own, take inventory of the apps that are represented by tiles on the Start screen. Decide which you never use, and unpin them. Locate apps you've acquired that you use often, and pin them to the Start screen. Move the tiles around so that the information or apps you need every day appear to the far left and you don't have to scroll to find them.

Changing the Start Screen Background and Color

Although you can't display pictures as backgrounds for the Start screen as you could in previous versions of Windows, you can choose a background pattern and color that appeals to you. It's a simple procedure to select your background and color from several preset selections.

Choose a Background and Color

1. Press Windows logo key+C.
2. Click Settings.
3. Click Change PC Settings.
4. Click Personalize.
5. Click Start Screen if it's not already selected.
6. Click a background.
7. Click a background color.

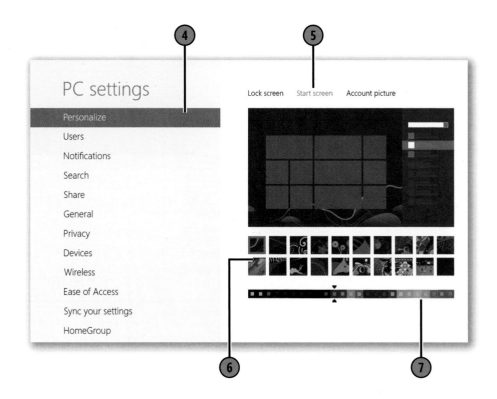

Personalizing the Lock Screen Background

The Lock screen appears when you first start your computer, when you put it to sleep using the Power setting, or when your computer goes to sleep after a period of inactivity. You can personalize this screen in few ways. This screen displays a background image that you can switch to another standard Windows Lock screen image, or you can use an image of your own.

You can also choose what notifications to display on the Lock screen, such as the time, date, and weather. To log in to Windows when the Lock Screen is displayed, you have to choose a user and enter a password. You can change the image that appears with each user name, using your own image or another picture of your choosing.

Choose a Lock Screen Image

1. Press Windows logo key+C.
2. Click Settings.
3. Click Change PC Settings.
4. Click Personalize.
5. Click Lock Screen if it's not already selected.
6. Click a picture.

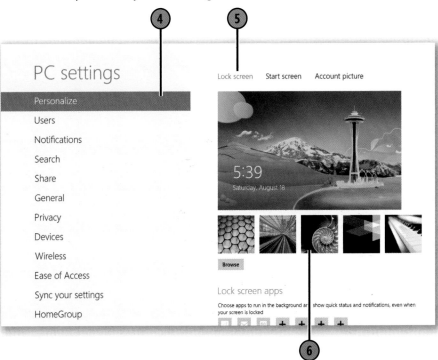

Tip

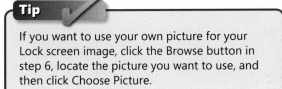

If you want to use your own picture for your Lock screen image, click the Browse button in step 6, locate the picture you want to use, and then click Choose Picture.

Setting Up Lock Screen Apps

By default, Windows 8 displays the date and time from the Calendar app, as well as notifications of any new messages from Messaging and Mail on your Lock screen. You can also choose to display the Weather app by using the steps in this section.

Choose Lock Screen Apps

1. Press Windows logo key+C to display charms.
2. Click Settings.
3. Click Change PC Settings.
4. Click Personalize.
5. Click Lock Screen if it's not already selected.
6. Click a button with a + symbol.
7. Click an app.

Tip

To stop displaying an item on the Lock screen, click an item in the Lock Screen Apps area and then click Don't Show Quick Status Here.

PC settings

Personalize
Users
Notifications
Search
Share
General
Privacy
Devices
Wireless
Ease of Access
Sync your settings
HomeGroup

Lock screen   Start screen   Account picture

5:39
Saturday, August 18

Browse

Lock screen apps

Choose apps to run in the background and show quick status and notifications, even when your screen is locked

Choose an app to display detailed status

Choose an app

Weather
Calendar
Messaging
Mail

Modifying the Account Picture

When you leave the Lock screen, you are presented with a picture and password field for any logged in user or, if nobody is currently logged in, for all users. If you assign a picture to a user account, that image will be displayed instead of a simple silhouette. Adding a picture for each account is a nice way to personalize Windows and quickly find your own account in a group of users.

Select an Account Picture

1. From the PC Settings screen (see steps in previous task), click Personalize.

2. Click Account Picture.

3. Click Browse.

4. Click Go Up if you want to find a picture in another folder.

5. Click an image.

6. Click Choose Image.

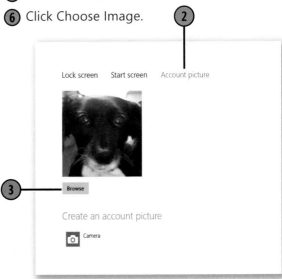

See Also

You can create a picture password that's required to log in to Windows 8. This feature requires a touchscreen computer; you assign a picture and then specify the touchscreen gestures you use with the picture to log in. See "Creating a Password Picture" on page 74 for more about setting up this feature.

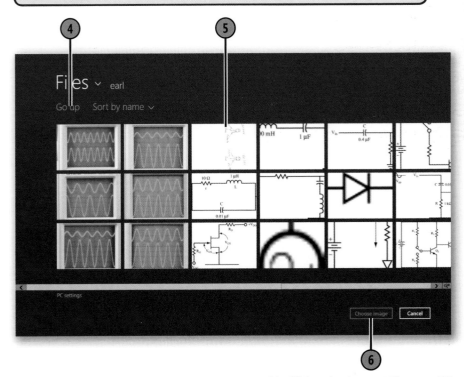

Putting Shortcuts on the Desktop

You can place shortcuts on the desktop to access frequently used documents or applications. This is the desktop equivalent of pinning tiles to the Start screen. After you create a shortcut, you simply double-click the shortcut to open a document or app.

Create a Desktop Shortcut

1. Click the File Explorer button on the desktop taskbar.

2. Locate the folder, document, or application you want to create a shortcut for.

3. Right-click the item, and choose Create Shortcut from the menu that appears.

4. Click and drag the shortcut for the item that appears in File Explorer onto your desktop.

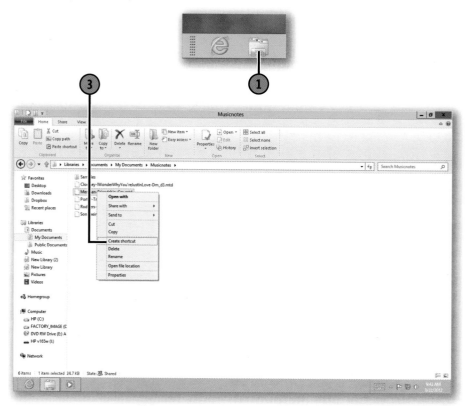

Tip

To delete a shortcut, right-click it and choose Delete. To rename a shortcut, right-click and choose Rename from the same shortcut menu.

See Also

See "Using the File Explorer Ribbon" on page 130 for more about locating files and folders by using File Explorer.

Choosing a Desktop Theme

The appearance of the desktop is a bit more customizable than the Start screen, allowing you to select preset themes or even save your own themes based on your choice of background and color. Themes apply several personalization settings at once, which means that changing the look of your desktop is quicker and easier in Windows 8.

Choose a Theme

1. Display the desktop.
2. Right-click the desktop, and choose Personalize.
3. Click a theme to preview it.
4. Click the Close button.

Tip

You can save your own themes. Under the category of My Themes, whatever theme you are using, including any changes you have made to it, appears as Unsaved Theme. If you want to save that theme, click it and then click Save Theme. In the dialog box that appears, give the theme a name and then click Save.

Tip

You can get more themes on the Internet. With the Personalization window shown in step 3 displayed, click Get More Themes Online. The Windows 8 Themes webpage opens in your browser. Use the theme categories or search feature to find a theme you like, and then click Save to download and save the theme. The theme is now available through the Personalization window of the Control Panel.

Changing the Desktop Background

You can choose your own background for your desktop to give it a more personalized look. Windows provides some attractive pictures along with the alternative option to use a solid color for your background, or you can use any image or photo you have available in your Pictures library.

Select a Different Background

1. Display the desktop.

2. Right-click the desktop, and choose Personalize from the menu that appears.

3. Click Desktop Background.

4. Click an image to select it, or click the Picture Location drop-down list and choose from categories such as Solid Colors or your Pictures Library.

5. When you locate a background you like, click Save Changes.

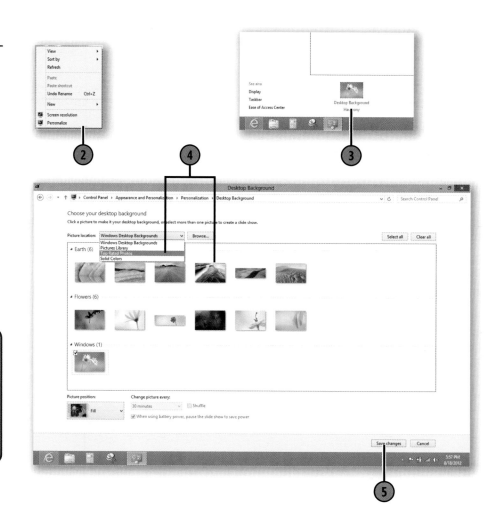

See Also

Section 17 provides information about working with photos and how to find and save photos on your computer. After you save a photo to your computer, you can use the Browse button in the Personalization, Desktop Background window to locate and use it as your desktop background.

Changing the Desktop Color Scheme

Windows allows you to change the color of window borders and the taskbar. You can choose from a variety of preset colors and also enable the Transparency feature, which gives an attractive glowing effect to these desktop elements.

Change Windows Color and Transparency

1. Right-click the desktop, and choose Personalize.

2. Click Color.

3. Click a color scheme to preview it.

4. Click Save Changes.

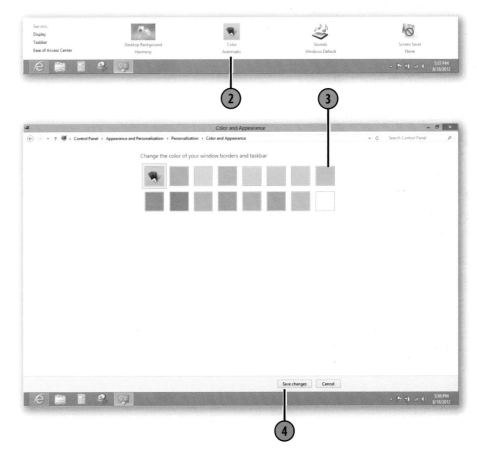

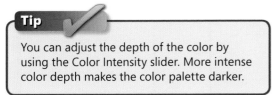

Tip

You can adjust the depth of the color by using the Color Intensity slider. More intense color depth makes the color palette darker.

Adjusting Screen Resolution

Other settings in the Control Panel affect both the Start screen and desktop. For example, you can apply higher screen resolution settings to improve the clarity of onscreen images. Higher resolutions make the overall screen elements smaller, while lower resolutions make them bigger. Use resolution to adjust what's on screen so that things are comfortable for you to view and read.

Change Screen Resolution

1. Right-click the desktop, and choose Personalize.

2. Click Display.

3. Click Adjust Resolution.

4. Click the Resolution drop-down list, and use the slider to choose a resolution.

5. Click Apply.

6. Click Keep Changes in the dialog box that appears.

7. Click OK.

8. Click the Close button.

Tip

The higher the resolution numbers, the crisper the image on your screen. However, some resolutions can distort the proportions of your screen so that items appear out of perspective. Also, not all monitors support the highest resolutions.

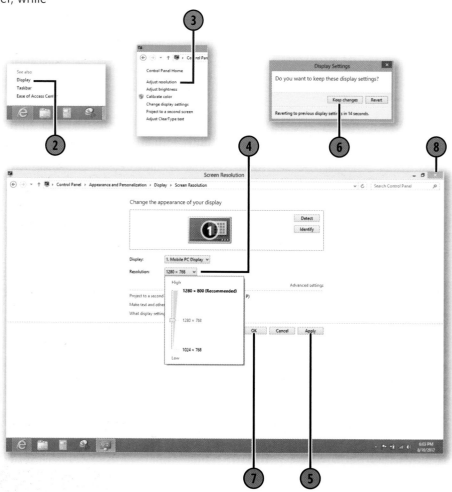

6

Working with Users and Privacy

Through an Internet connection, your computer and the information that users create on it are vulnerable to various forms of abuse, including the downloading of malware such as viruses and the risk that websites and programs can access your personal information and location.

Windows 8 has several built-in protections against these threats that are easy to set up and manage, if you know what to look for. Windows Firewall stops files from being downloaded to your computer without your knowledge. Windows Defender is a feature that guards against spyware and malware, which include programs that can be downloaded to your computer that watch your activities or corrupt your data.

To keep information private, you can set up multiple user accounts on your computer. Each user can save certain settings and content. Users can each have a unique picture, password, and even a PIN, which helps them log on to your computer quickly and easily. You can manage user account settings to enhance your computer's security and set up Account Control Settings to notify you when there is an attempt by another user to install programs on your computer or change your Windows settings. Finally, you can use Family Safety controls to manage the content that younger users can access.

Enabling Windows Firewall

Windows Firewall is a feature that checks information being sent or downloaded from the Internet or another network to your computer. Firewall then either allows access or rejects the access, depending on the settings you have applied. I strongly recommend that you turn on Windows Firewall. However, a firewall doesn't replace the need for antivirus and anti-spyware software; your computer can be exposed to threats via avenues other than the Internet and networks.

Turn On Windows Firewall

1. From the Start screen, begin to type **Control Panel**.

2. When the search result displays the Control Panel app, click it.

3. Click System And Security

4. Click Windows Firewall.

5. Click Turn Windows Firewall On Or Off.

6. Select the Turn On Windows Firewall option in the Private Network or Public Network settings, or turn on both if you log on to public hot spots.

7. Click OK.

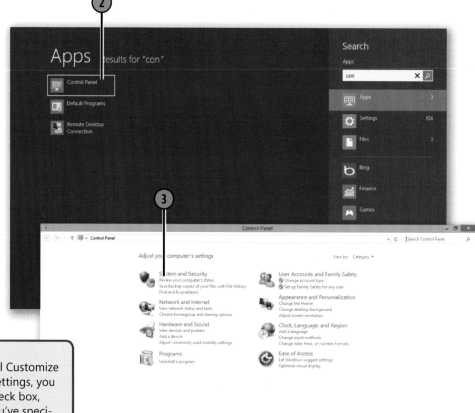

Tip

If you want extra security, in the Windows Firewall Customize Settings dialog box, under the Private Network settings, you can select the Block All Incoming Connections check box, which blocks any incoming connection even if you've specified that the connection is safe. By default, the option for notifying you when Windows blocks a program is selected, but you can turn that off if you don't want a notification.

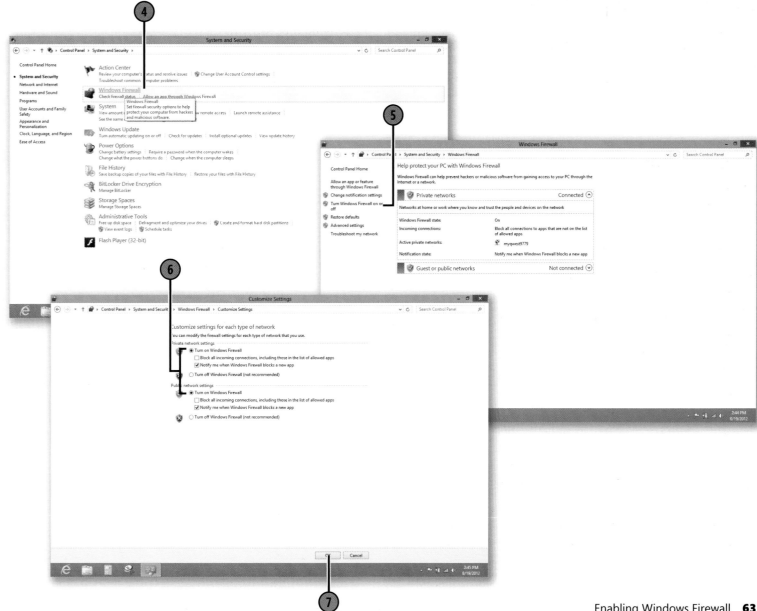

Allowing Apps to Access Your Computer

You can use privacy settings in Windows 8 to allow programs to access your location or your name and account picture. For example, you might want a mapping app to have access to your location so that it can display directions from where you are to another location. Or, you might want to allow websites you go to regularly to recognize you and greet you by name when you visit.

Allow Access to Your Location

1. Press Windows logo key+C.

2. Click the Settings charm.

3. Click Change PC Settings.

4. Click Privacy.

5. Click the On button for the Let Apps Use My Location setting.

Tip ✓

There is some danger associated with allowing access to your location. If you or your child are concerned that an individual might want to know where you are at any point in time, you are more at risk if you carry a laptop or tablet device with you, and you might consider blocking this access. However, for most people, this feature simply adds convenience when using certain applications.

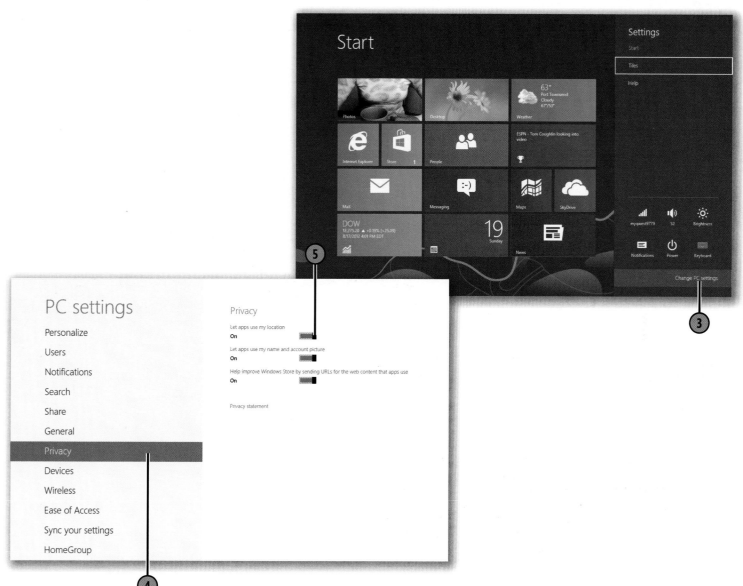

Allow Access to Your Information

1 Press Windows logo key+C.

2 Click the Settings charm.

3 Click Change PC Settings.

4 Click Privacy.

5 Click the On button for the Let Apps Use My Name And Account Picture setting.

6 Click the On button for the Help Improve Windows Store By Sending URLs For The Web Content That Apps Use setting.

See Also

Network security can help you control who has access to your files and data. When you create a network, you establish your network security type. See Section 19, "Working with Devices and Networks," for more about network security settings.

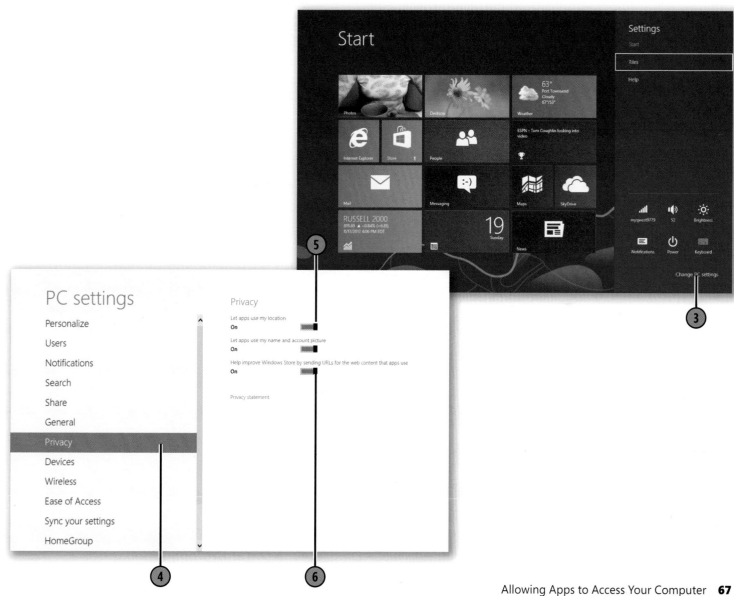

Settings

Start

Tiles

Help

myqwest9779   52   Brightness

Notifications   Power   Keyboard

Change PC settings

Start

Photos   Desktop   63°
Port Townsend
Cloudy
67°/53°
Weather

Internet Explorer   Store   1   People   ESPN – Tom Coughlin looking into
video

Mail   Messaging   Maps   SkyDrive

RUSSELL 2000
819.89 ▲ +0.84% (+6.85)
8/17/2012 4:06 PM EDT   19
Sunday   News

PC settings

Personalize

Users

Notifications

Search

Share

General

Privacy

Devices

Wireless

Ease of Access

Sync your settings

HomeGroup

Privacy

Let apps use my location
On

Let apps use my name and account picture
On

Help improve Windows Store by sending URLs for the web content that apps use
On

Privacy statement

Setting Up Windows Defender

Windows 8 provides built-in protection against viruses and spyware with a feature called Windows Defender. Integrated with Internet Explorer, Windows Defender scans files you download from the Internet to detect threats. When turned on, the program automatically provides real-time protection against threats, stopping malware from being downloaded. You can also run manual scans any time you like. Remember that this free protection is akin to other free anti-malware protection you can find online. It is good, but if you want more robust security—for example, if you often visit unknown websites or often download files to your computer—you might consider purchasing an anti-malware software program.

Set Up Virus and Spyware Protection

1. From the Start screen, begin to type **Windows Defender**.

2. When the Windows Defender app appears in the Search results, click it.

3. Click the Settings tab.

4. Make sure the Turn On Real-Time Protection check box is selected.

5. Click Save Changes.

6. Click the Close button.

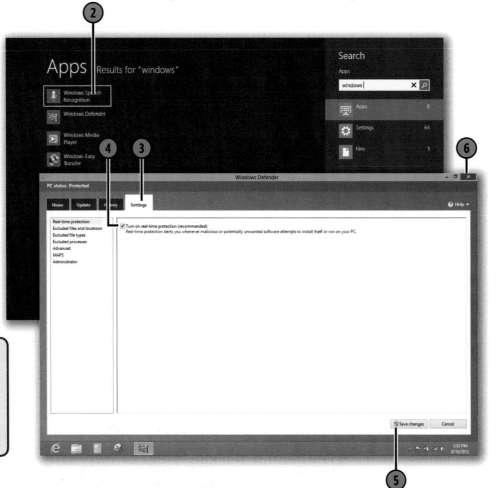

Tip

Updates are performed automatically when real-time protection is turned on. However, these updates occur only every few days. To run a manual update at any time, click the Update tab of Windows Defender and then click the Update button.

Scan for Malware

① From the Start screen, begin to type **Windows Defender**.

② When the Windows Defender app appears in the Search results, click it.

③ On the Home tab, click either the Quick or Full scan option.

④ Click the Scan Now button.

⑤ When the scan is completed, check to see what threats, if any, were detected.

⑥ Click the Close button.

Try This!

You can customize your scan. Follow the steps in this task, but at step 3, click the Custom Scan option. When you click the Scan Now button, you can select check boxes for the drives you want to scan. For example, you can scan only your hard disk, any DVD or removable/external drive attached to your computer, or all drives. Click OK to run the scan.

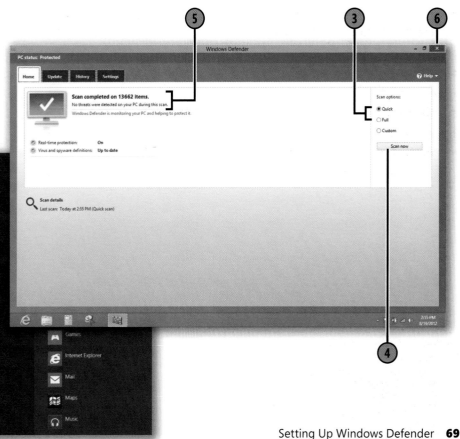

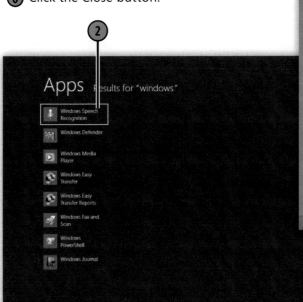

Setting Up User Accounts and Passwords

If more than one person works on your computer, you might want to set up several user accounts. Each user account can have unique settings and store different documents. You can also password-protect these accounts and assign a user photo so that each user has a private computing experience. You can set up a user account by using a Windows Live account. (You have one if you have a Live, Hotmail, or MSN email account, or you can create one when you create a new user.)

When you set up your computer for the first time, you create your own user account and you are set up as the account administrator, meaning that you have the ability to make and change any settings. Any user accounts you set up subsequently are set up by default as Standard users, meaning that they can't make changes to more sensitive settings dealing with features such as security and privacy.

Create a New User

1. Press Windows logo key+C.
2. Click the Settings charm.
3. Click Change PC Settings.
4. Click Add A User.
5. Enter an email address.
6. Click Next.
7. Click Finish.

Tip

When you set up user accounts for children, you might want to set some parameters for how they can use the computer and its Internet connection. See "Turning on Family Safety" later in this chapter for help with this.

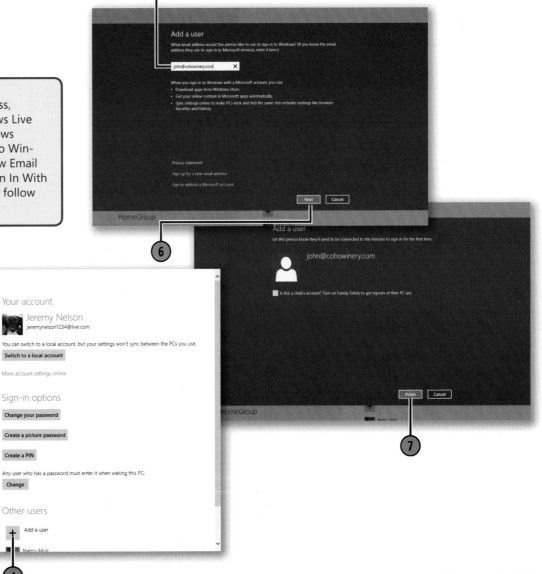

Tip

If you enter a non-Windows Live address, you might be asked to create a Windows Live account after step 6. To create a Windows Live account or to log on locally with no Windows Live ID, tap the Sign Up For A New Email Address or Don't Want This User To Sign In With A Microsoft Account links in step 5 and follow the instructions.

Set a User Password

1. Press Windows logo key+I.
2. Click Change PC Settings.
3. Click Users.
4. Click Change Your Password.
5. Enter your old password.
6. Enter your new password and confirm it.
7. Click Next.
8. Click Finish.

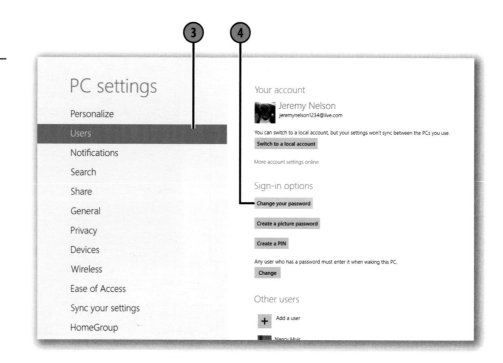

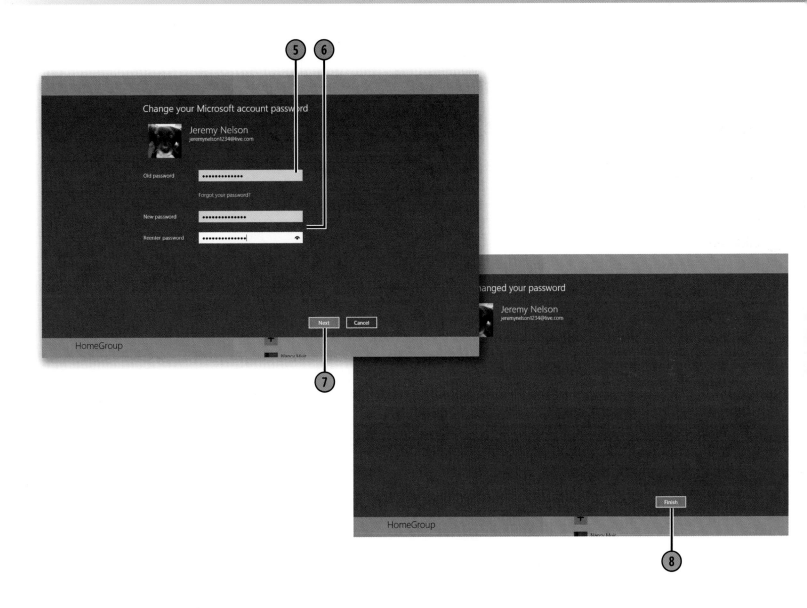

Creating a Password Picture

If you have a touchscreen computer, you can set up a password picture. In this procedure, you choose a password picture and then record three onscreen gestures associated with the picture, which you repeat to log on.

Select a Picture

① Go to PC Settings. (Press Windows logo key+I and click Change PC Settings.)

② Click Users.

③ Click Create A Picture Password.

④ Enter your password.

⑤ Click OK.

⑥ Click Choose Picture.

⑦ Click a source for your picture, such as Sample Pictures.

⑧ Click Go Up if you want to go to another folder.

⑨ Click a picture.

⑩ Click Open.

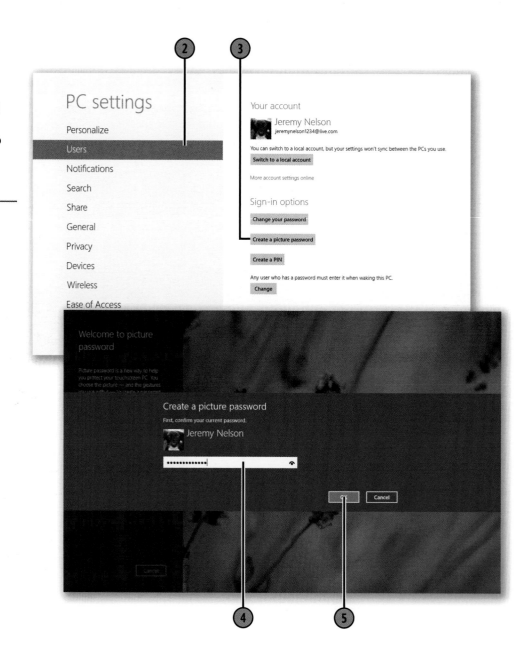

Set Up Password Gestures

① Click Use This Picture.

② Using your touchscreen, add three gestures to your picture by swiping across it in any position or direction.

③ When prompted on the next screen, repeat the three gestures.

④ Click Finish.

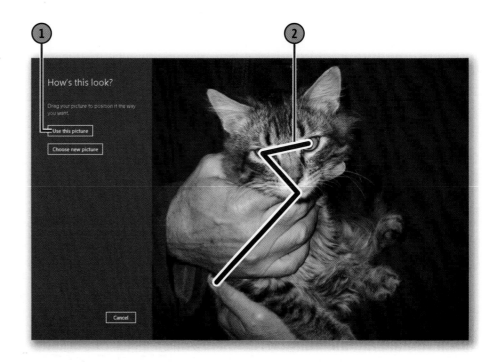

Tip ✓

Don't forget your password gestures; Microsoft has no record of them. The best procedure is to make a note of the password gestures and keep that note away from your computer so that anyone trying to access data on your device can't find it.

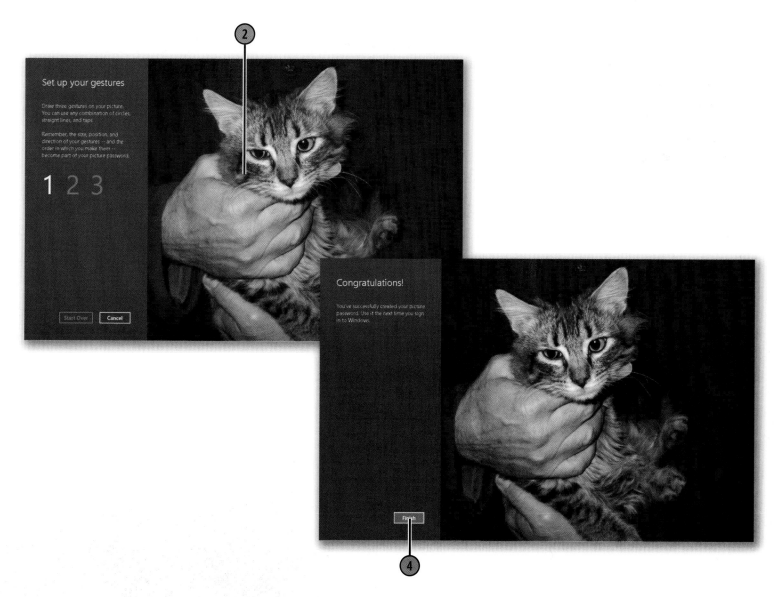

Set up your gestures

Draw three gestures on your picture.
You can use any combination of circles,
straight lines, and taps.

Remember, the size, position, and
direction of your gestures -- and the
order in which you make them --
become part of your picture password.

1 2 3

Start Over   Cancel

Congratulations!

You've successfully created your picture
password. Use it the next time you sign
in to Windows.

Finish

Creating a PIN

Entering an email address and password might require that you type 20 or 30 characters, which takes a bit of your precious time. What if you could log on to Windows 8 with just 4 characters? That's what a PIN does for you: it's a shorthand way to log on, and it's easy to create.

Set Up a PIN

1. Open PC Settings. (Press Windows logo key+I and click Change PC Settings.)
2. Click Users.
3. Click Create A PIN.
4. Enter your password.
5. Click OK.
6. Enter a PIN and then confirm it.
7. Click Finish.

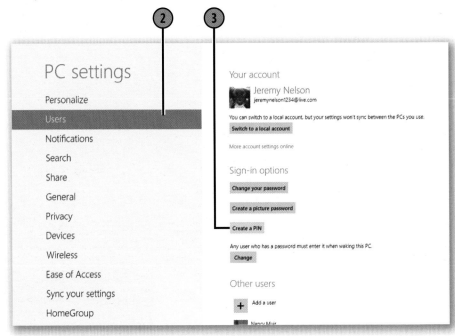

Tip

Just as with a password, make your PIN hard to guess, even though the characters are limited in number. For example, don't use part of your phone number, street address, or date of birth, because these pieces of information are often publicly available. If you need something that's not totally random to help you remember it, use a number that represents a date or year that has special meaning known only to you, or part of a phone number from 10 years ago.

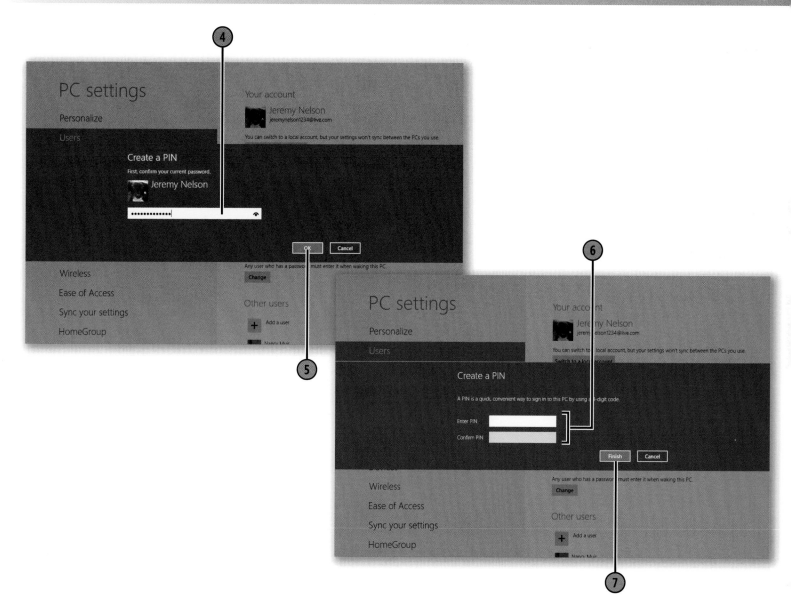

Switching Among User Accounts

When you have set up more than one user account on your Windows 8 computer, you will want to switch among them. For example, you might have one account for you and one for your spouse. With separate accounts you can each make your own settings and save your own documents and limit access to those documents with a personal password or PIN. You change to a different account from the lock screen.

Log In as a Different User

1. Click Windows logo key+L to display the lock screen.

2. Drag the screen upward to reveal the user logon screen.

3. Click the arrow to the left of the user picture.

4. Click another user picture.

5. Enter the user password.

Tip ✓

If you have administrative privileges on your Windows 8 device, you can use the User Accounts And Family Safety option in the Desktop Control Panel to manage accounts. From there, you can set up Family Safety for each account, change the account type, delete accounts, and even change the password for local accounts.

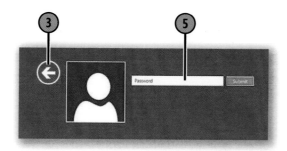

Managing User Account Control

You can use the User Account Control Settings dialog box to set up, by user, how Windows notifies you before programs are installed on your computer or when there are attempts to make changes to your Windows settings. You can choose a level of protection that works best for each user. If only one user on the computer has administrative level permissions, it can be useful to set up the Always Notify level of account control for that person so that she knows when other users try to make changes.

Change User Account Control Settings

1. From the desktop, open the Control Panel.

2. Click System And Security.

3. Click Action Center.

4. Click Change User Account Control Settings.

5. Drag the slider to the setting you prefer, with Always Notify being the most secure and Never Notify being the least secure.

6. Click OK.

7. Click the Close button.

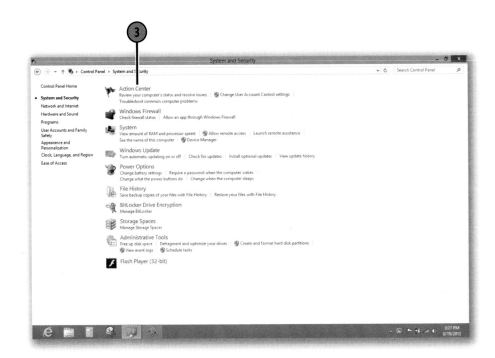

See Also

For more information about making settings for individual users, see "Create a New User," earlier in this section.

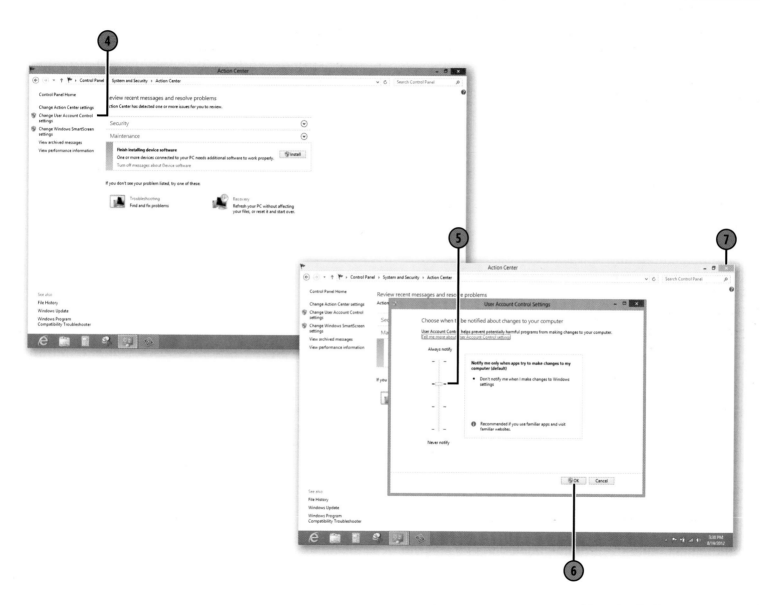

Turning On Family Safety

If children use your computer, consider setting up Family Safety controls through their user accounts. These controls allow you to make different settings for each child. For example, you might want to limit the time a teen spends online so that homework gets done, or block a younger child from using certain programs on your computer.

Turn On Family Safety

(1) From the desktop, open the Control Panel.

(2) Click Set Up Family Safety For Any User.

(3) Click a user.

(4) Under Family Safety, click the On, Enforce Current Settings option.

(5) Click Close.

See Also

See the next task for managing individual Family Safety control settings. For information about using Internet Explorer settings for a safer browsing experience, see Section 12, "Going Online with Internet Explorer 10."

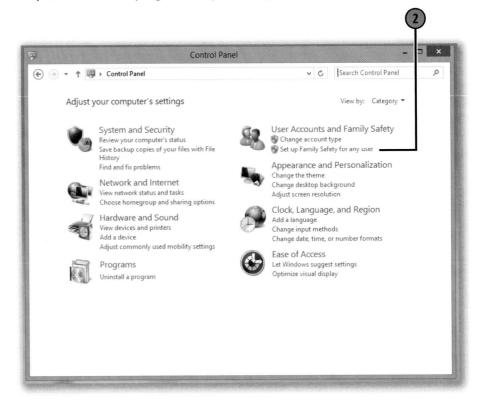

Working with Family Safety Settings

With Family Safety settings, you can set time limits so that you can control the amount of time and the time periods for which your child can use the computer. You can choose which games children can access by rating, content, or title. Finally, you can block specific programs from being used by your child on your computer.

Set Up Web Restrictions

1 In the Control Panel, click Set Up Family Safety For Any User.

2 Click a User for whom Family Safety is turned on.

3 Click Web Filtering.

4 Click to allow access to all websites.

5 Click to block some websites or content.

6 Click to allow only specified websites on the Allow And Block List. (Click the Edit The Allow And Block List link to specify allowable URLs.)

7 Click to choose a web filtering level.

8 Click the Close button.

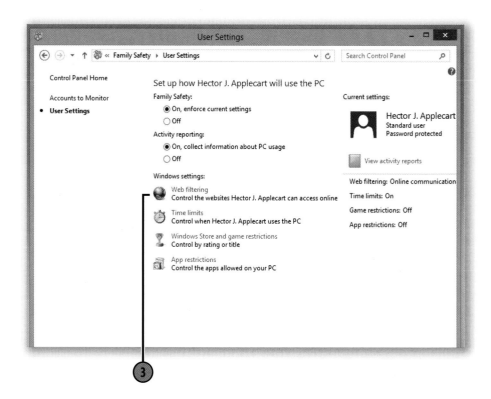

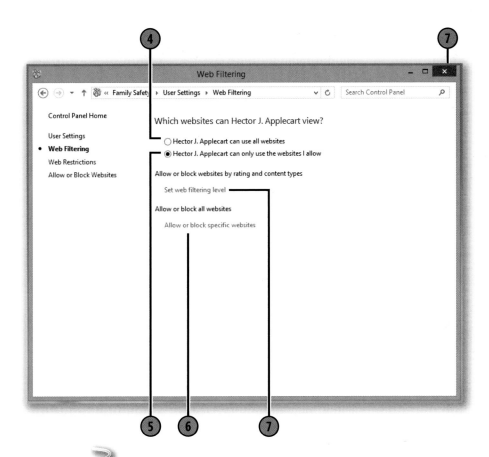

Try This!

Make a list of the types of content that make sense for each of your children to be able to access and review those choices periodically as they grow up. For example, you might choose to change settings for the junior high student to appropriate settings for a high school student when the time comes to help him "graduate" to a more mature phase.

Set Time Limits

① From the Family Safety dialog box, click on a user for whom Family Safety is turned on.

② Click Time Limits.

③ Click Set Time Allowance.

④ Click User Can Only Use The PC For The Amount Of Time I Allow.

⑤ Click the corresponding fields to set up the number or hours and minutes the user can use the computer on weekdays and weekends.

⑥ Click Close.

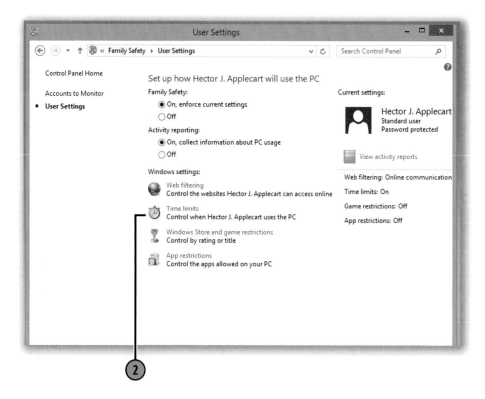

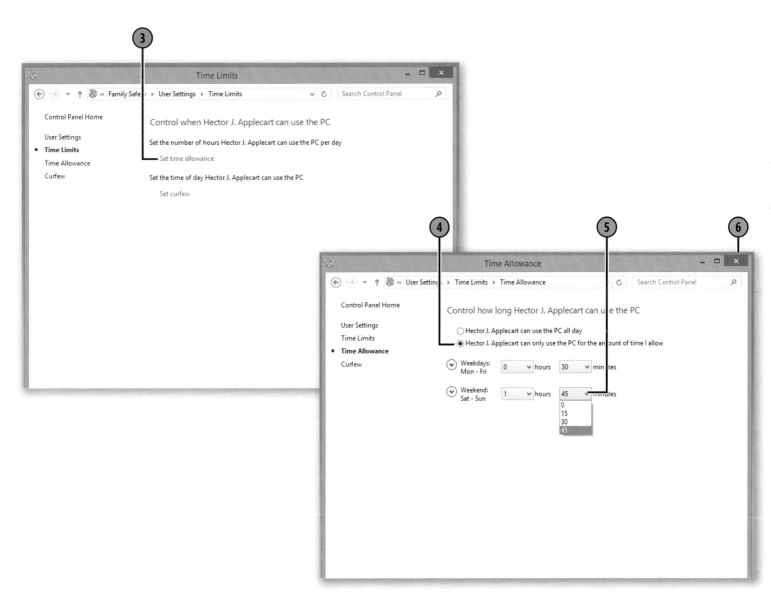

Set Up Games

1 In the Family Safety dialog box, click a user for whom Family Safety settings are turned on.

2 Click Windows Store And Game Restrictions.

3 Click the first option, "User" Can Play All Games And View All Windows Store Apps, if you don't want the user to play games; if you leave this setting selected, use the Allow Or Block Games And Windows Store Apps By Rating link to make additional settings.

4 If you prefer to allow the user to use some games, click Set Game And Windows Store Ratings.

5 Click to allow or block games with no rating.

6 Click a rating level.

7 Click the Close button.

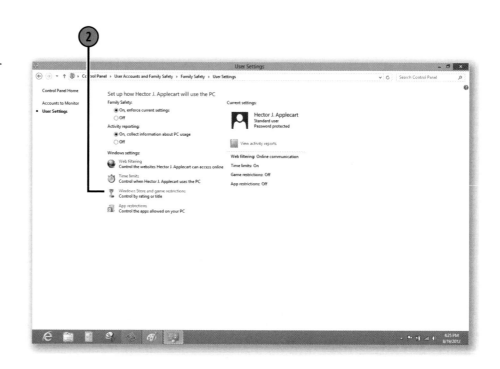

Tip

If your children are into online games, take a look at Section 9, "Working with Apps," for more about playing games online, including some safety tips.

Tip

It is possible to stop users from working with certain apps by using Family Safety. For example, if you use a program for your work and don't want to risk having your child open your work and make changes to it, you might want to use this control. If you want to restrict access to certain apps on your computer, on the Family Safety screen displayed in step 2 of this task, click a user and then click Program Limits. Click the option for allowing use only of certain programs, and then on the list that appears, click to select any installed programs. Click OK to set this control.

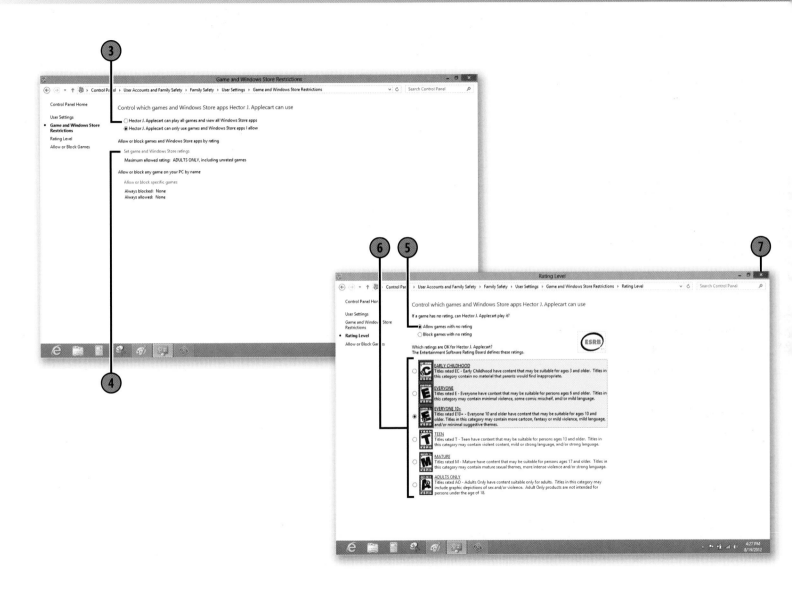

7

Working with Accessibility Settings

To provide input to your computer, you use a mouse, keyboard, or your fingers on a touchscreen. To make input easier if you have hearing, dexterity, or vision challenges, you can make good use of a variety of accessibility settings in Windows 8.

For example, if you have trouble hearing, you can adjust the volume of your system; all volume controls in software programs and Internet apps are then set against that system volume level.

If you have vision challenges, you can control the contrast setting on your screen and turn on a setting to make everything on bigger.

Finally, if hand dexterity is a challenge, there are two features you should check out. The first, caret browsing, is a setting by which you can use your keyboard to navigate a webpage rather than your mouse, if you find the keyboard easier to use. If you prefer an entirely hands-off approach, you can also explore a new means of input, Speech Recognition, to speak text and instructions to your computer.

Switching from a Right to Left-Handed Mouse

A common mouse setting involves switching which buttons control right-click and left-click settings. Changing these can help left-handed individuals use their mouse and its right and left buttons more intuitively. In addition, experts recommend that those who use a computer often switch these settings to avoid carpal tunnel pain.

Switch from Right to Left-Hand Clicking

1. On the Start screen, begin to type **Control Panel**.

2. Click the Control Panel app.

3. Click Hardware And Sound.

4. Under Devices And Printers, click the Mouse link.

5. Click the Buttons tab.

6. Select the check box labeled Switch Primary And Secondary Buttons to change the left button to perform actions typically performed by a right-click.

7. Click OK.

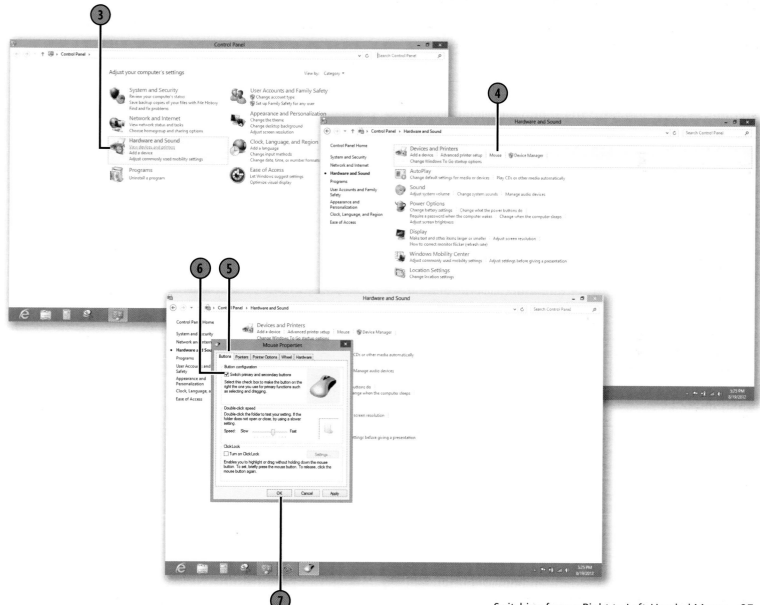

Adjusting Double-Click Speed and Indicator Motion

If double-clicking to get some things done presents a challenge because you have trouble clicking fast enough, you can adjust the speed at which the mouse responds to a double-click. Windows can then recognize a double-click even though the individual clicks occur at a longer interval. You can also modify how fast the mouse indicator moves across your screen so that you can follow its path more easily.

Change Double-click Speed and Motion Setting

1. In the Control Panel (on the Start screen, type **Control Panel** and then click Control Panel), under Devices And Printers, click the Mouse link.

2. On the Buttons tab, drag the slider in the Double-Click Speed category to set the speed at which you want to double-click your mouse to initiate an action.

3. Click the Pointer Options tab.

4. Drag the slider in the Motion setting section to adjust how fast or slow the pointer moves on your screen in response to mouse movements.

5. Click OK.

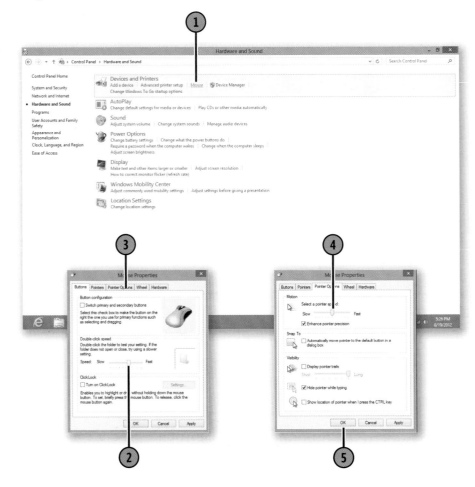

Setting Up Snap To and Display Pointer Trails

To make selections in dialog boxes simpler, you can set up your mouse pointer to move to the default selection, which is usually the most common option that people work with. You can also choose to display a trail on your pointer as it moves across the screen. If you typically have trouble locating your indicator on the screen, the shadowy trail can make it more visible.

Set Up Snap To and Pointer Trails

1. In the Control Panel (type **Control Panel** on the Start screen, and then click Control Panel), click Hardware And Sound.

2. Under Devices And Printers, click the Mouse link.

3. On the Pointer Options tab, select the Snap To check box to move the pointer to the default choice in dialog boxes.

4. Select the Display Pointer Trails check box and then use the slider to select long or short mouse pointer trails.

5. Click Apply.

6. Click OK.

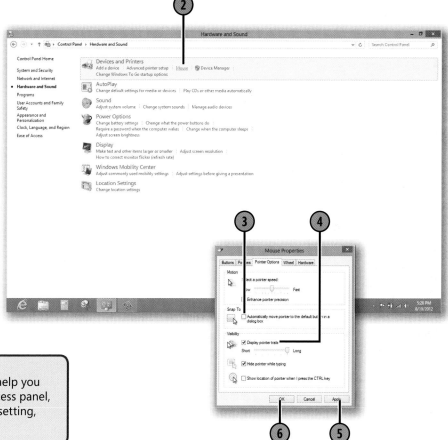

Tip

You can adjust the thickness of the mouse cursor to help you spot it more easily. In PC Settings, on the Ease Of Access panel, click the Cursor Thickness drop-down list and click a setting, with 1 being the thinnest and 20 being the thickest.

Adjusting Touch Keyboard Settings

You have some control over how your touch keyboard functions; by making changes to keyboard settings you can make the touch keyboard easier to use. Commonly used settings include choosing the language for your keyboard when entering text and how your gestures are interpreted by the touchscreen. These settings will not appear if you have a computer without a touchscreen.

Control Touch Keyboard Settings

1. Press Windows logo key+I to display Settings panel.

2. Click Change PC Settings.

3. Click General.

4. Change the On/Off sliders to change any of the following self-explanatory settings:

   - Show Suggestions As I Type

   - Add A Space After I Choose A Text Suggestion

   - Add A Period After I Double-Tap The Spacebar

   - Capitalize The First Letter Of Each Sentence

   - Use All Uppercase Letters When I Double-Tap Shift Key

   - Play Key Sounds As I Type

   - Make The Standard Keyboard Layout Available

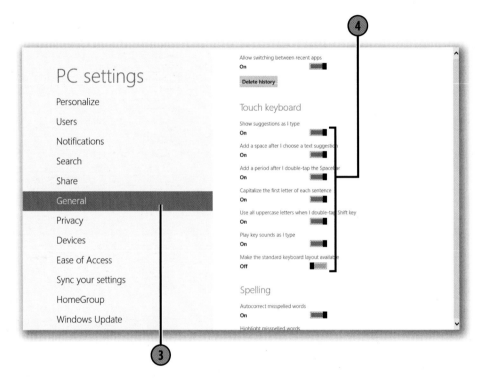

Adjusting System Volume

One of the computer settings that people commonly like to change is the system volume. If you've ever watched a TV show on your computer and cringed as the commercials come on full blast, you know what I mean. Changing system volume is therefore front and center on the Settings panel.

Adjust System Volume

 Press Windows logo key+I to display Settings.

 Click the Volume button.

 Drag the slider to raise or lower volume.

Tip

You can mute sound on your computer at any time by clicking at the bottom of the volume slider. Drag this slider up to unmute the computer.

Tip

If you want separate control over system volume and the volume of system sounds (such as an alert that an email has arrived), display the desktop, and then in the taskbar, click the Volume button. At the bottom of the Volume settings, click the Mixer button, and then use the sliders to adjust the volume for different types of sounds.

Controlling Contrast and Screen Size

If you have difficulty seeing items on your screen, you might want to customize some visual settings. To help those with vision challenges, Windows provides settings for adjusting the screen contrast and making the items displayed on your screen bigger. Turning on High Contrast essentially turns the background of your screen black and the text white.

Change Contrast and Adjust Screen Size

1. Press Windows logo key+I.
2. Click Change PC Settings.
3. Click Ease Of Access.
4. Click the On/Off slider for High Contrast.
5. Click the On/Off slider for Make Everything On Your Screen Bigger.

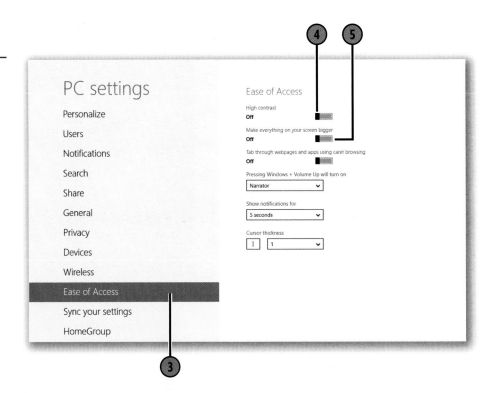

> **Tip**
>
> If you use a laptop computer, it's often the case that the function keys that run along the top of your keyboard provide a way to make your screen brighter or dimmer. To use these keys, first tap the key labeled Fn (usually located in the lower left of your keyboard) and, without letting go of the Fn key, press the function key for brightness (often it shows the image of a sun).

Turning On Caret Browsing

Caret browsing is a setting by which you can use your keyboard to navigate a webpage rather than using your mouse. When you turn this feature on, you can use the Home, End, and Page Up, Down, Right, and Left keys to move from link to link or to select text. Caret browsing can help the mouse challenged enjoy their Web browsing experience more.

See Also

Section 12, "Going Online with Internet Explorer 10," provides more information about using the Internet Explorer web browser and various techniques you can use for navigating the web.

Turn On Caret Browsing

1. Press Windows logo key+I.

2. Click Change PC Settings.

3. Click Ease Of Access.

4. Click the On/Off slider for Tab Through Webpages And Apps Using Caret Browsing.

Working with Speech Recognition

Speech recognition has been around for several years, and the technology has made great progress in its ability to recognize voices and accents and deliver more accurate results. The Windows Speech Recognition feature has become a practical alternative to entering text or commands with a keyboard, although you will still have to review text for misunderstood words and clean up punctuation a bit.

To get started with Speech Recognition, you first have to turn the feature on; then, you can make various settings for how it works.

Start Speech Recognition

1. On Start screen, begin to type **Control Panel**.
2. Click the Control Panel app.
3. Click Ease Of Access.
4. Click Start Speech Recognition.
5. Click Next to move on from the Welcome screen. (See the next task.)

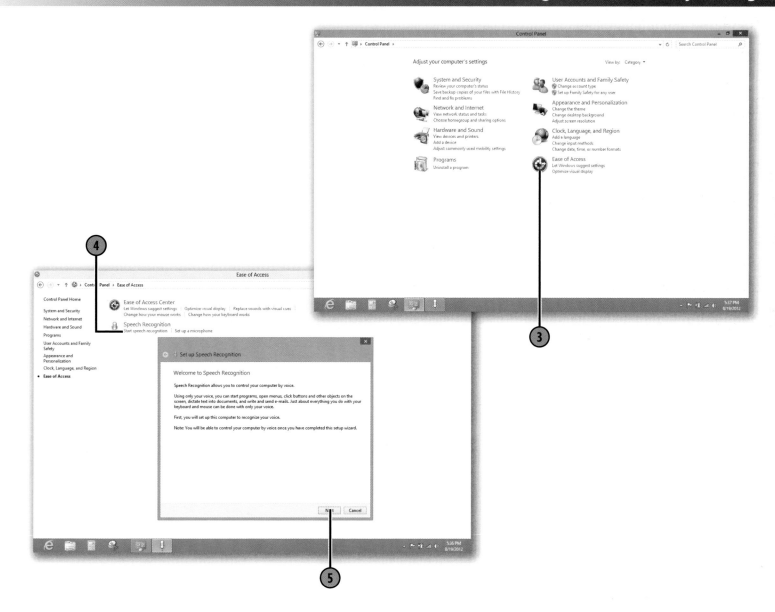

Set Up Speech Recognition

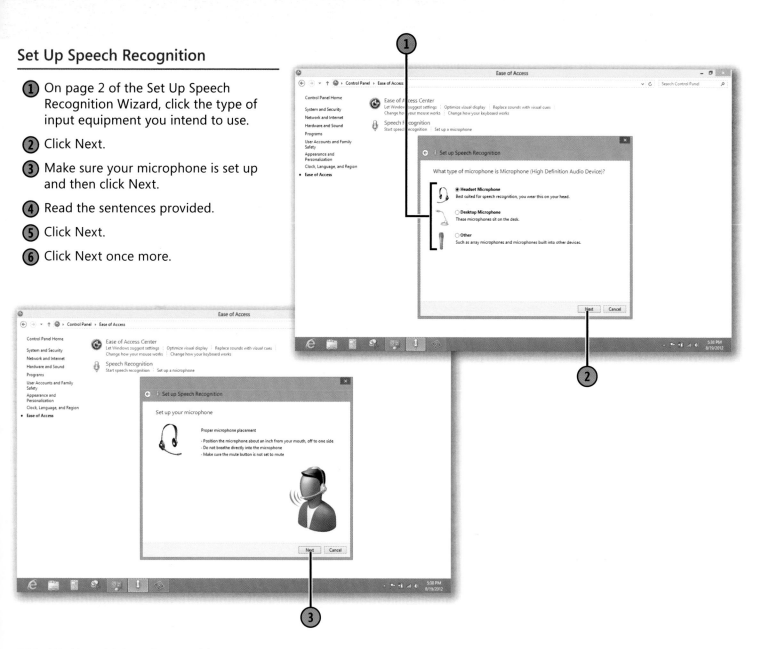

① On page 2 of the Set Up Speech Recognition Wizard, click the type of input equipment you intend to use.

② Click Next.

③ Make sure your microphone is set up and then click Next.

④ Read the sentences provided.

⑤ Click Next.

⑥ Click Next once more.

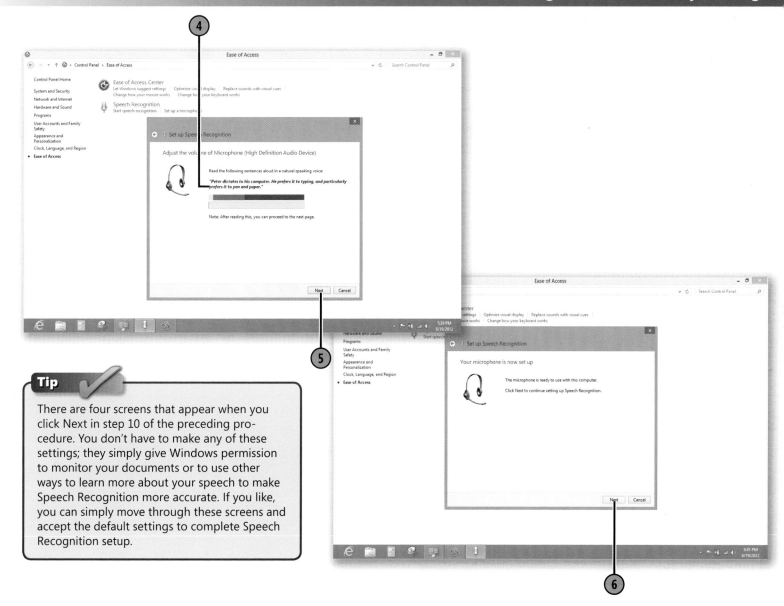

Tip

There are four screens that appear when you click Next in step 10 of the preceding procedure. You don't have to make any of these settings; they simply give Windows permission to monitor your documents or to use other ways to learn more about your speech to make Speech Recognition more accurate. If you like, you can simply move through these screens and accept the default settings to complete Speech Recognition setup.

Use Speech Recognition

After you have set up Speech Recognition, you can try it out. To do this, you'll need to have a headphone attached to your computer to speak text and commands and you'll need to learn to use the Speech Recognition controls.

1. After setting up Speech Recognition (see previous task), return to the Ease Of Access dialog in the Control Panel (follow steps 1-4 of the previous task) and click Start Speech Recognition.

2. Click the Microphone button on the Speech Recognition controls.

3. Speak commands into your microphone, such as "Open WordPad."

4. Begin to speak a sentence.

5. Click the Microphone button again to turn Speech Recognition off.

6. Click the Close button on the Speech Recognition controls to close the program.

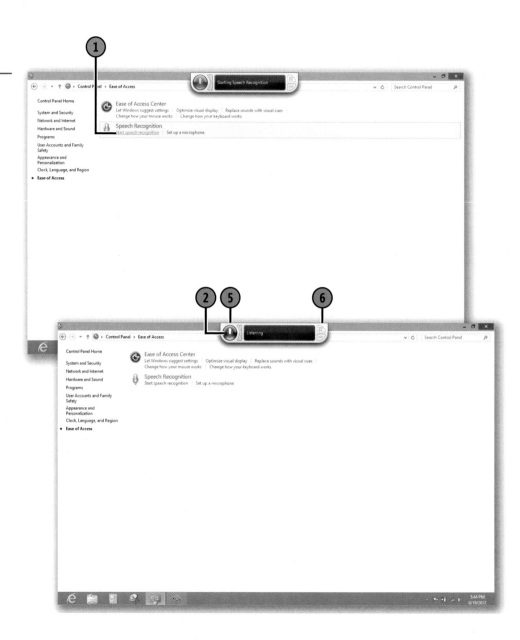

8

Searching

The Integrated Search feature of Windows 8 is one of its most powerful new features. *Integrated* refers to the ability of Windows 8 to search not only your computer but also the Internet to find a wide variety of results. Finding what you need is simple because you don't have to open up a search feature or screen. You simply begin typing a search term with the Start screen displayed. Windows 8 then brings up a Search screen with results and tools that help you narrow your search.

Using this advanced searching technique, you can find more than files on your computer: you can locate Windows administrative tools and settings, emails, photos, music, and much more.

Windows 8 also offers settings that help you limit your search to certain categories, giving you a lot of control over your search results.

Searching on the Start Screen

Searching in Windows 8 is the most intuitive way to search you've ever experienced. You simply begin to type and search results appear. If you've used traditional search methods by which you have to locate a search feature, click in a text box, and then type, you will need to get used to this new approach.

Use Integrated Search

1. On the Start screen, begin typing a word, such as **windows**.

2. Complete typing the term in the search box that appears.

> **Tip**
>
> To clear the search box but stay on the Integrated Search screen, click the X to the right of the search box.

Using the Search Charm

You can access the Search charm on either the Start screen or from the desktop by displaying the charms. This method also takes you to the Integrated Search screen.

Open the Search Charm

1. Press Windows logo key+C.

2. Click the Search charm.

3. Begin to type a search term.

Locating Files, Apps, and Settings

To help you focus your search so that you can find just what you're looking for, Integrated Search provides more tools than a traditional search feature. That's because the search feature reaches beyond Windows 8 and searches the Internet, too, assuming you have an Internet connection. This feature lets you search for items such as emails, contacts, photos, videos, games, items in the Windows Store, files, installed apps, music, maps, and even administrative tools and settings for Windows 8.

Search for Items

1. With Integrated Search open (see one of the previous two tasks), enter or complete your search term.

2. Click any category beneath the search box, such as Files, Maps, or Store, to narrow your search.

3. When the results appear, you can click another category to get different results.

4. To open any of the results, just click an item.

Try This!

Enter a city, such as Seattle, in the search box. Click Maps to get a map of the city. Next, click Weather to see the weather forecast for the city. Tap Music, and it's probable that Windows will locate a musical selection with the city name included. This is a great way to get all kinds of information about a new place you're visiting!

Tip

If your results are too detailed, click the Pan and Zoom tool in the lower-right corner of the screen to go to an alphabetical overview. Click one of the letters to go to results that begin with that letter.

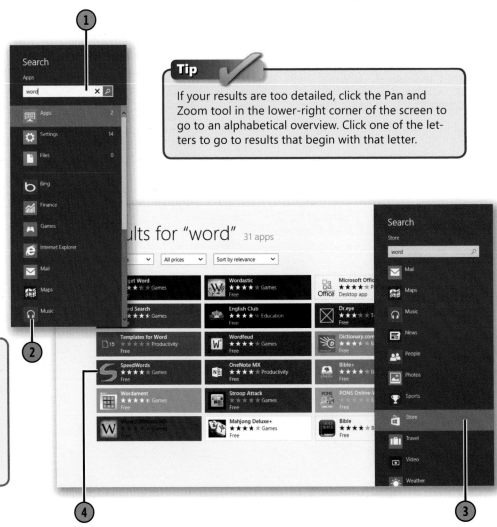

Customizing Search

There are a few settings you can apply for the Search feature that can make your searches more efficient. You can also make settings to keep your search history private. By deleting your search history, you ensure that nobody else can discover what you search for.

Customize How Search Works

1. Press Windows logo key+I.

2. Click Change PC Settings.

3. Click Search.

4. Click Delete History to clear your search history.

5. Click the slider to turn the Let Windows Save My Searches As Future Search Suggestions feature off or on.

6. Click the slider to turn the Show the Apps I Search Most Often At The Top feature off or on.

7. Press the Windows logo key to return to the Start screen.

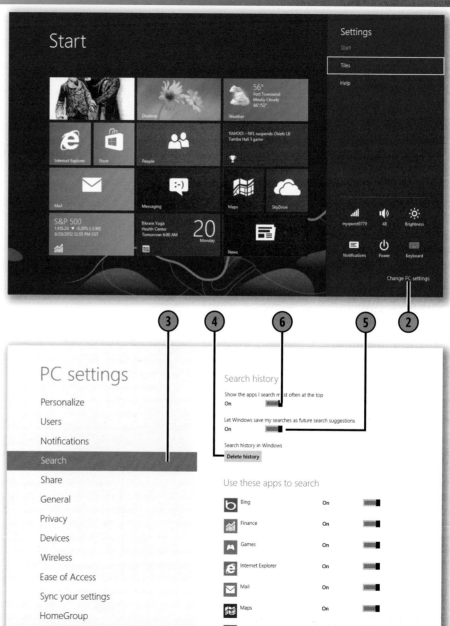

Setting Which Apps to Use for Searching

The wealth of search options in Windows 8 is "impressive; however, you might prefer not to have the Search feature return results in every category. For example, you might prefer not to search the Windows Store but to go there from the Store app on the Start screen to shop. Or you might prefer not to get video results, especially if you are working on a Windows 8 tablet with a battery that might run down quickly when playing videos. Setting which apps to include in a search is simple.

Choose Apps for Searching

1. Press Windows logo key+I.

2. Click Change PC Settings.

3. Click the On/Off slider for any app to control whether Search should include it in searches.

4. Press the Windows logo key to return to the Start screen.

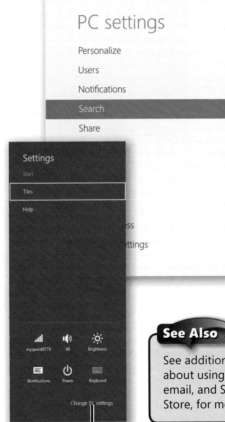

> **Tip**
>
> Remember that certain apps, such as Weather and Store, require that you have access to the Internet to return results. If you don't have access, the search feature will search only your computer hard disk for matches in apps, files, and settings categories.

> **See Also**
>
> See additional sections in this book, such as Section 12 about using Internet Explorer, Section 13 about using email, and Section 14 about shopping at the Windows Store, for more search options from within those apps.

Working with Apps

9

Everything today is about apps, computer applications that have become very modular and customizable. The Windows 8 Start screen displays several pre-installed apps, such as Calendar, Music, Weather, Internet Explorer, and Xbox LIVE Games. In addition to the apps displayed on the Start screen by default, other pre-installed apps are available that you might be familiar with from previous versions of Windows, such as Paint, WordPad, and Sticky Notes. (These were referred to as Windows Accessories in previous versions.)

You can also install desktop applications such as Microsoft Excel or Quicken from Intuit. These more robust desktop applications have several features in common, which you'll learn about in this section.

One application that comes with Windows 8, WordPad, has similarities to many desktop applications, such as Microsoft Word or Excel. It has a combination of menus and a ribbon toolbar, and you can enter, format, and edit text and objects. In this section, you'll see how to use WordPad and some of the other common application features, including how to open apps, format text, insert objects, print, save files, close, and uninstall apps.

Opening Desktop Apps

Apps on the Start screen can be relatively simple—for example, a calendar, the weather, or a music or video player. Apps that open on the desktop are the more traditional applications, such as those in the Microsoft Office suite. These can be pinned to the Start screen, but they open within the desktop environment. These desktop applications typically offer full-featured tools, such as menus, toolbars, and the ability to save and open documents.

Open WordPad

1. On the Start screen, begin typing **WordPad**.

2. Click WordPad in the search results.

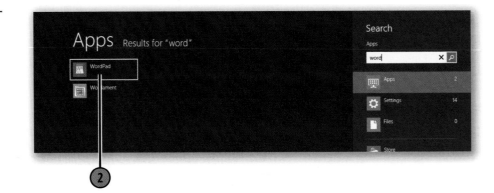

Tip

You can also right-click on the Start screen to display the All Apps button. You can then use the scrollbar at the bottom of the screen to locate the app you want to open.

Using Menus

Menus have been around in software for a long time. You click a menu, and a list of commands appears. Click a command, and a few things can happen. A dialog box might be displayed offering a group of settings. A submenu might be displayed offering additional commands. Finally, the software might take an action, such as opening a new, blank document.

Use the File Menu in WordPad

① On the Start screen, type **WordPad**.

② Click WordPad in the search results.

③ Click File.

④ Click commands to open a new document, open an existing document, save a file, and so forth.

⑤ Hover your mouse over a command that has an arrow to its right to open a submenu of additional commands.

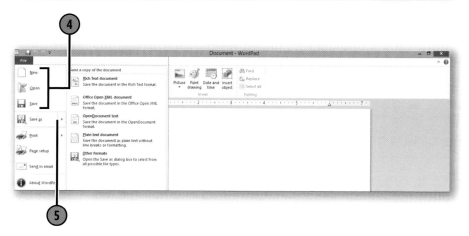

Using Toolbars/Ribbons

Many apps and more robust desktop applications typically provide graphical tools that you can click to get things done. In some programs, these are arranged on a toolbar; in Microsoft programs such as WordPad, they are arranged on various tabs on a *ribbon*. The ribbon includes a File tab that displays commands for working with documents, such as Open, Save, and Print. In addition, there is usually a Home tab that offers the most commonly used editing tools to format text. WordPad also offers a View tab on which you can use tool buttons to zoom in and out, display a ruler, and more.

Explore the WordPad Ribbon

1. With WordPad open, click the File tab.

2. Click Save.

3. Type a name for the document.

4. Click Save.

5. Click the View tab.

6. Click the Zoom In button.

7. Clear the Ruler check box to hide the Ruler.

8. Select the Ruler check box to display it again.

9. Click the Home tab.

10. Click the Date And Time button.

11. Select a format.

12. Click OK.

13. Click the Save button.

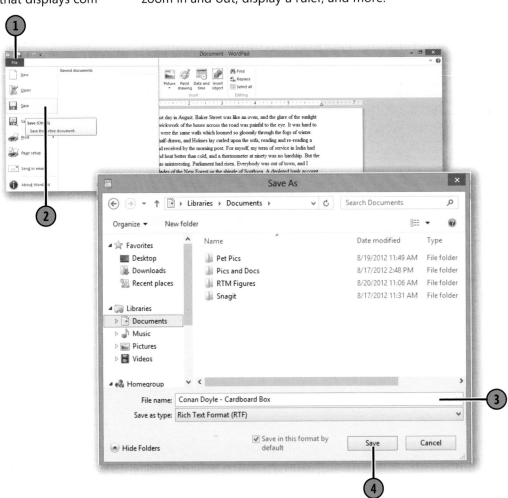

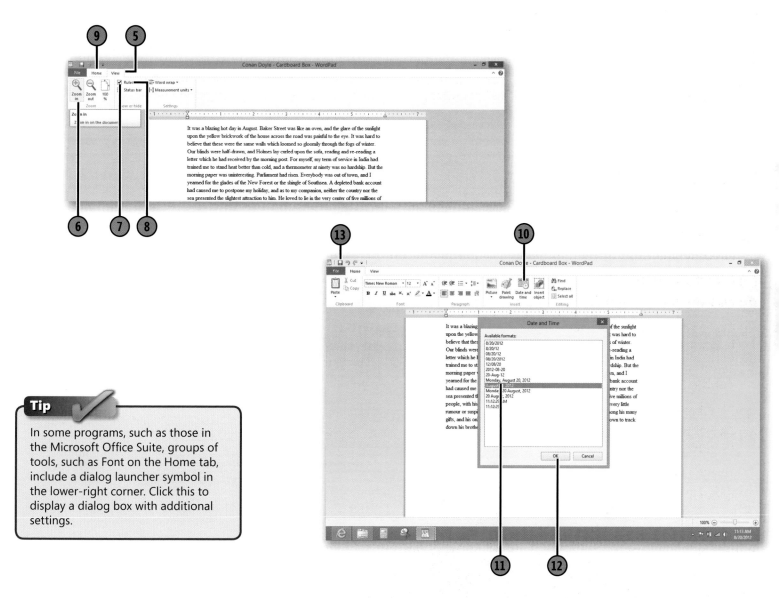

In some programs, such as those in the Microsoft Office Suite, groups of tools, such as Font on the Home tab, include a dialog launcher symbol in the lower-right corner. Click this to display a dialog box with additional settings.

Entering and Formatting Text

Many apps and desktop style applications require that you enter text. For example, you can enter text in an email message in the Mail app, in a Microsoft Word or Excel document, or in a text field in Messaging. After you enter text, tools are often available to format the text with color or bold, italic, or underline effects. There are other tools with which you can adjust spacing between lines of text or to align text across the page relative to the left and right margins.

Enter, Select, and Format Text

① With WordPad open, enter a few words of text.

② Click to the left of the text, and drag to the right or down to select some or all words.

③ Click Bold, Italic, or Underline buttons to apply those styles to the selected text.

④ Click the Font Color button and choose a color for your text from the drop-down palette.

⑤ Click to display the Font list and then click a different font to apply it to selected text.

⑥ Click to display the Font Size list.

⑦ Click a size to apply it.

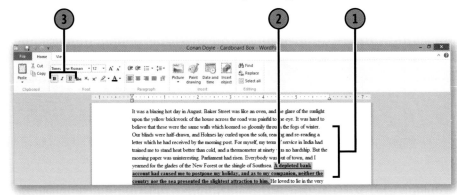

Tip

If you apply a font other than the default font style to text, be aware that if you or somebody else opens the document on a different computer or a computer with a different operating system, or as a document on the web, not all fonts will be available. Other programs try to substitute available fonts, and the results might or might not appeal to you. Sticking to more common fonts such as Verdana, Times New Roman, and Arial might be your safest bet.

...g and Copying to Windows Clipboard

...elp you place a copy or to move a piece of text or an object such as a picture to another location, Windows provides a feature called the Clipboard. This is a holding area for text and objects that you cut (remove) or copy from a document.

An item stays on the Clipboard for a time until you find a new location in the document or in another document where you want to paste it. If you cut or copy several items, the oldest item will eventually be permanently deleted.

Use Windows Clipboard

1 With WordPad open and text entered, select some text.

2 Right-click and select Cut or Copy on the options panel.

3 Click File, New.

4 In the new document, click the location where you want the text to appear.

5 Right-click, and click Paste on the context menu.

Try This!

To copy an object such as a picture, select it by clicking on it; handles appear around its edges. Follow the same procedure for cutting or copying text outlined here to move or copy the item. After you place the item in a document, you can make it larger or smaller by dragging the handles on its edges, and in some programs, you can edit a picture in other ways, such as cropping to a smaller area.

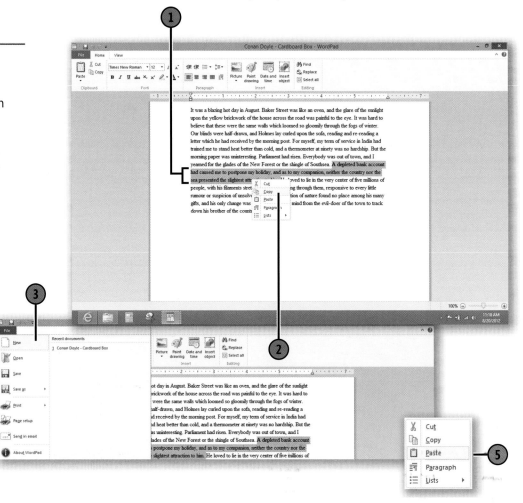

Inserting Objects

In many applications, you can insert a copy of an object, such as a graphic element like a photo or clip art (a collection of illustrations, photos, and animations that come with some applications such as Microsoft Word) into a document without having to use the copy and paste method.

Insert a Picture

① With WordPad open, click the Home tab.

② Click Picture.

③ Double-click a folder to open it and display images. (The Pictures folder opens by default, and any pictures you've saved or downloaded are likely to be in that folder.)

④ Click a picture.

⑤ Click Open.

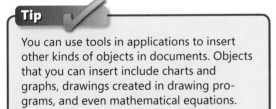

Tip ✓

You can use tools in applications to insert other kinds of objects in documents. Objects that you can insert include charts and graphs, drawings created in drawing programs, and even mathematical equations.

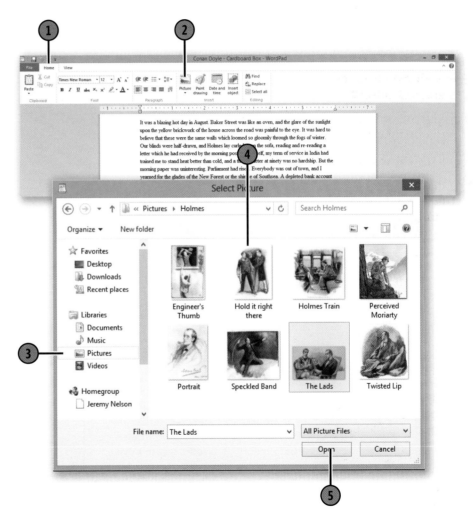

a Document

In many applications and apps you can print your documents or webpages. For example, you can print a memo from WordPad, an email from Mail, or a webpage displayed in a browser such as Internet Explorer. From desktop style applications such as WordPad, you use settings in a Print dialog box to print an open document. Make sure that you have a printer connected to your computer first!

Apply Settings and Print a Document

1. With WordPad open, click File.

2. Click Print.

3. Click the printer you want to print to, if it's not selected by default.

4. Click to select a range of pages (optional).

5. Click and choose a number of copies to print.

6. Click to collate copies (to print sets of pages from first to last).

7. Click Print.

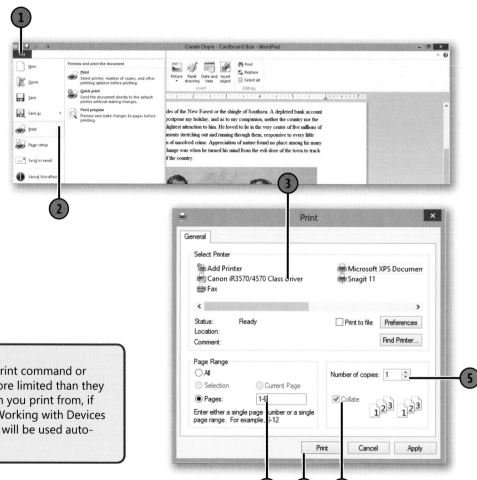

> ### Tip
>
> Apps such as Mail and Internet Explorer offer a Print command or button; however, the print options are usually more limited than they are with desktop applications. Whatever program you print from, if you've set up a default printer (see Section 19, "Working with Devices and Networks," for more about this), that printer will be used automatically when you print.

Saving a File

After you have entered some content in a document, it's a good idea to save the file on a regular basis so that you don't lose your work. You can save a document file to your computer hard disk or to external storage such as a USB flash drive or DVD. When saving for the first time, you can give the file a name and choose a format to save it to; the application's native format is the default. You can also save a copy of the file with a different name or in another location to create a backup copy in case the original is damaged.

Save a File

1. With a new WordPad document open, click File.

2. Click Save.

3. Click to select a library or folder to which to save the document.

4. Enter a document name.

5. Select a different document format, if necessary.

6. Click Save.

Tip

If you want to save a copy of a file you've previously saved, in step 2 you would click Save As, choose a location to save the file to, give it a new name if you like, and save it. You can't save two files with the same name in the same location; you have to either overwrite the original file or rename one of the files.

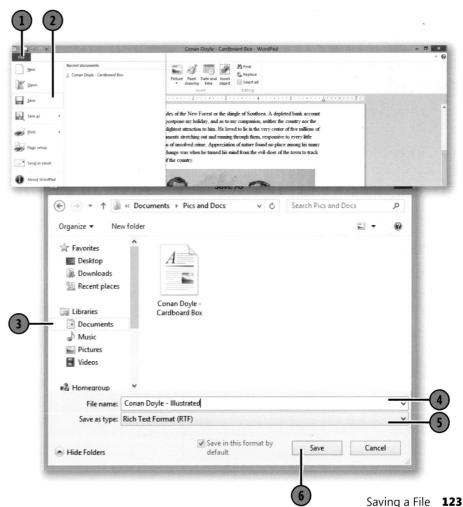

Exploring Games

On the Start screen, you will find a Games tile. This takes you to xBox Games, which includes some spotlighted games and access to the xBox 360 Games Store and the Windows Games Store. You can play standalone games or play with others online. In Games, you can set up a game avatar and profile to use with game apps, as well as view your achievements and gaming friends. In this task, you set up your Avatar and Profile in the Games app. Once that's done, download a game and try your hand at it.

Setting Up Your Avatar and Profile

1. On the Start screen, click the Games tile.

2. Scroll to the left to display the Avatar settings.

3. Click Create Avatar.

4. Click to select an avatar to use.

5. Click to adjust the shape of the avatar.

6. Click Save; note you can customize the avatar at any time by clicking Customize Avatar and changing settings for clothing, jewelry, shoes, and so on.

7. Click Edit Profile.

8. Enter your name, motto, location, and bio.

9. Click Save.

Tip

When creating your profile, to protect your privacy, don't share too much information. Don't make your location too specific (for example, by giving your address); just give a state or region. Don't reveal many personal details in your bio.

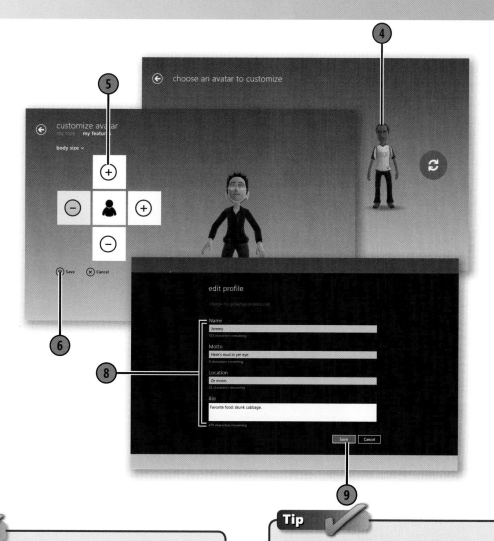

Closing Apps

The way by which you close apps changes with Windows 8. In some cases, you don't close an app, you just return to the Start screen by pressing the Windows logo key on your keyboard or by clicking the Start screen charm. In others, especially with more traditional desktop applications, you click the standard Close button. Finally, with apps such as Weather and Maps, you can drag (or swipe if you have a touchscreen) downward to close an app.

Close an App

① With a desktop application open, such as WordPad, click the Close button.

② With a Start screen app open, such as Weather, click the top of the screen and drag downward.

Uninstalling Apps

Although computers today give you lots of memory to fill up with apps, images, and documents, if you no longer need an app, it's still a good idea to uninstall it. After you uninstall an app, you have to reinstall it to use it again, which requires either that you have a disc or discs to install it from or that you re-download it to your computer. If you've decided that you don't need to use an app again, follow these simple steps to uninstall it.

Uninstall an App

① On the Start screen, right-click an app.

② Click Uninstall.

③ Click Uninstall.

Tip

Note that when you click Uninstall in step 2, Windows might display a list of related apps that will be uninstalled along with the app you selected. Pay careful attention to this list so that you don't uninstall something you need.

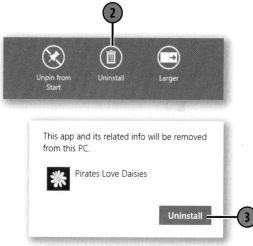

10 File Management

You accomplish both work and play on a computer by using computer files. For example, those files might hold the software applications you work with, the documents you create in a word processor or spreadsheet, a game, or your favorite song or movie.

Windows 8 organizes your files into folders and libraries. There are several pre-defined libraries such as Pictures and Documents, but you can add others. Within these libraries are folders containing individual files.

You use the File Explorer app to perform the following tasks:

- Find files you've saved on your computer or on an external storage device such as a USB stick.
- Create new folders and move or copy files among them.
- Delete files you no longer need.
- Back up files in a file history or on an external storage device so that you have an extra copy for safekeeping.
- Create compressed versions of files that are smaller and easier to store and send to others.

Using the File Explorer Ribbon

In previous versions of Windows, File Explorer was called Windows Explorer. New to File Explorer in Windows 8 is a ribbon of tools that you can use to work with your files and folders. If you've used previous versions of Windows, it's worth taking a moment to review the contents of the new ribbon. The tabs on the ribbon provide different types of tools, including the following:

- On the Home tab, you can copy and paste items, organize and delete them, create new libraries and folders, and open or select files and folders.

- You can use the tools on the Share tab to send files to others or to share them with other users in your computer network.

The Home tab

The Share tab

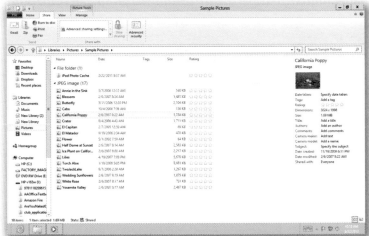

- On the View tab you can look at the contents of your drive in a variety of ways, showing specifics levels of detail and sorting the contents by criteria such as name, size, or date created.

- You can use the File tab to access Favorite Places, open a new File Explorer window, clear your recent items or address bar history, or modify options for how you work with folders.

The View tab

The File Menu

> **Tip**
>
> Content-specific tabs, such as Picture Tools, appear when you have selected certain types of content.

Using Libraries

The files and folders that contain files are organized into libraries. Several pre-existing libraries are provided for you, including Documents, Music, Pictures, and Videos. You can move files and folders among libraries, and you can create new libraries.

For example, you might want to move pictures you've downloaded from the Download folder into the Pictures library, or you might create a library for your artwork or one for documents associated with business clients.

Move Folders Between Libraries

① On the Windows desktop, click the File Explorer icon.

② Double-click a library to open it.

③ Click a folder and drag it to another library.

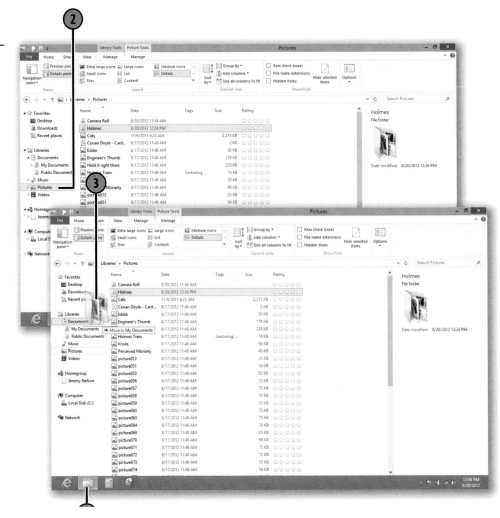

Create a New Library

1 With File Explorer open, click the Home tab and click Libraries.

2 Click New Item and then Library.

3 In the new library that appears with a placeholder name highlighted, enter a name for the library and press Enter.

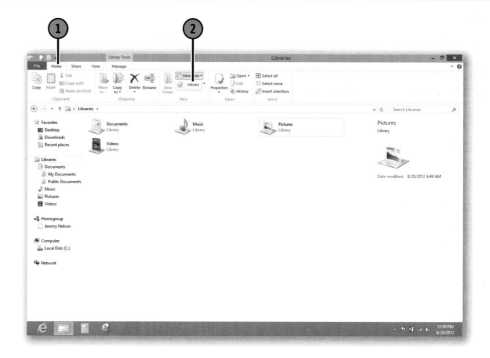

Tip

Assign unique and descriptive names to libraries so that you can easily find the folders and files within them.

Try This!

Use libraries for broader topics; you can create folders within the Documents library for narrower topics to keep libraries to a manageable number. For example, create a folder for house-related items. Then you should populate it with "sub-folders" for Budget, Renovations, Mortgage, and Insurance. Create folders within the Documents library for narrower topics, such as Gardening Tips, Association Minutes, or Holiday Address Lists.

Navigating File Explorer

File Explorer offers several ways to move among the libraries and folders on a drive. You can move up to a higher level—for example, from a subfolder to a folder or from a folder to a library of folders—or move back or forward to a previously viewed item. You can also display a list of recently viewed items.

Navigate Among Libraries

1. On the Windows desktop, click the File Explorer icon.

2. Click the Pictures library.

3. Click a folder.

4. Click the Up arrow to the left of the address bar to go up one level in the file/folder hierarchy.

5. Click the Back arrow to display the Pictures folder contents again.

6. Click the drop-down arrow to the right of the Forward button to display a list of items you've recently viewed in File Explorer.

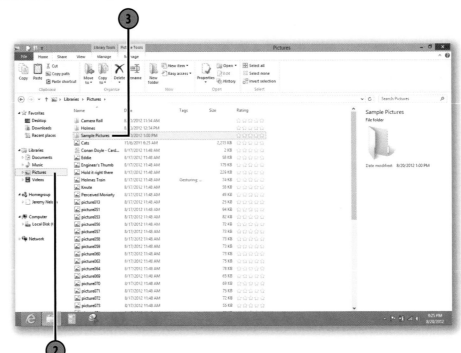

Tip

With a folder open in File Explorer, you can click Properties on the Home tab and then click Properties on the drop-down menu. The window that appears will give you information about the folder, such as how many files and subfolders it contains, the date it was created, and whether the folder is shared with others.

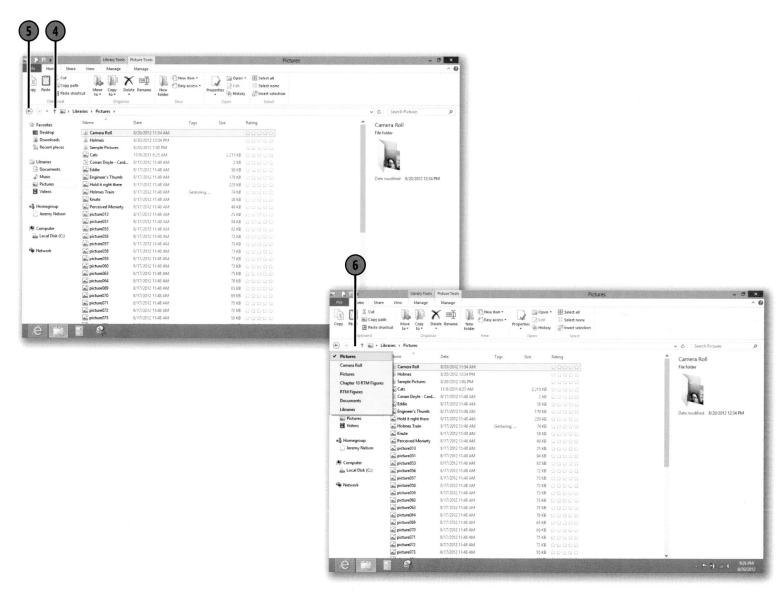

Finding Files and Folders with File Explorer

File Explorer organizes your files within folders and libraries. Because a file can be tucked into a folder or subfolder, you might have to hunt for it. One approach is to methodically move from library to folder to file through a logical hierarchy until you find the file. Another approach is to search for the file; the search results will take you directly to the file, no matter where it's located.

Locate a Folder in a Library

1. With File Explorer displayed, double-click a library to display its contents.

2. Double-click the folder that contains the file.

3. If the file is contained in a subfolder, double-click that folder to display its contents.

Tip

When you double-click a folder that contains subfolders, those subfolders are displayed in the leftmost pane of File Explorer. Any lower-level folders within any of those subfolders are displayed in the middle pane of File Explorer.

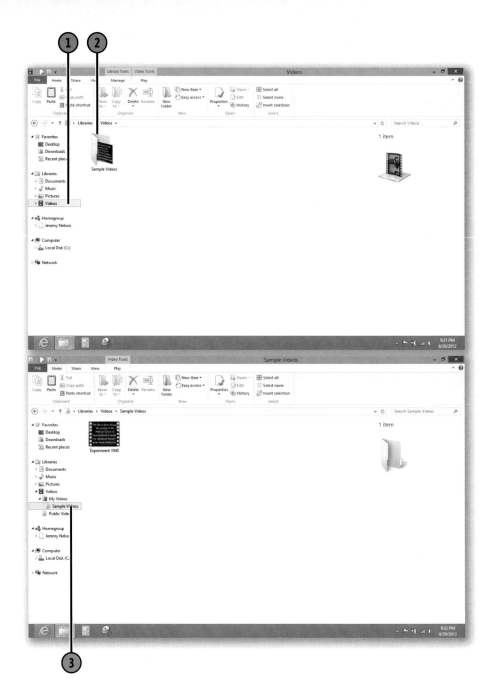

Search for Files and Folders

1 With File Explorer displayed, click in the search field.

2 Enter the name of the file; matching files are displayed as you type.

3 Double-click a file to open it.

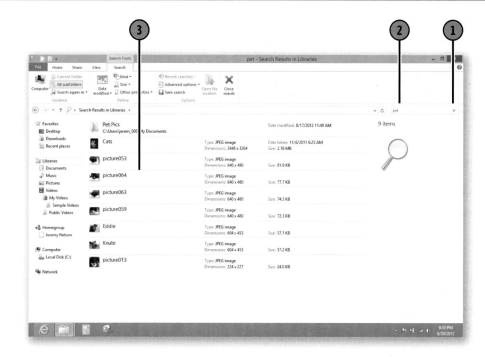

Changing Views in File Explorer

In File Explorer, you can choose among several views to see the items on your drive from different perspectives. For example, you might choose to view picture files as small icons of the pictures, or you might choose to see documents in a folder displayed in a detailed list that includes the file names, date modified, and size. The ability to display items in different layouts and grouped or sorted by certain criteria makes File Explorer an invaluable tool for navigating through the contents of your hard disk or an external storage device.

Use View Tab Tools

1. With File Explorer open, click the View tab.

2. Click the Details Pane button to display details about a selected item.

3. Click the Sort By button to display a menu of sort options.

4. Click a sorting option in the list.

5. Click the Group By button to display a menu of options for grouping content.

6. Click an item on the list to group contents.

7. Select a check box in the Show/Hide tools section to display file name extensions or show hidden items.

Tip

To hide an item such as a file or folder in File Explorer, click to select it, and then on the View tab, use the Hide Selected Items button to hide it from view. Select the Hidden Items check box to then display hidden files again.

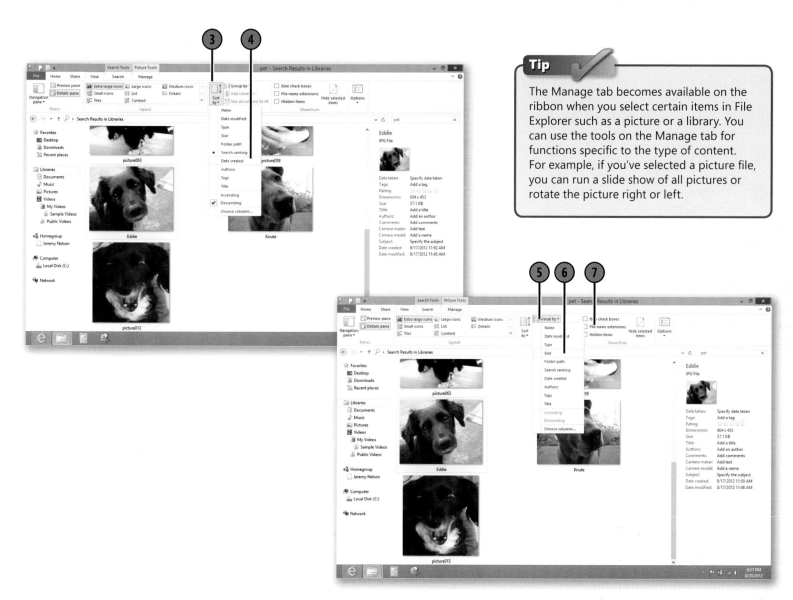

Tip

The Manage tab becomes available on the ribbon when you select certain items in File Explorer such as a picture or a library. You can use the tools on the Manage tab for functions specific to the type of content. For example, if you've selected a picture file, you can run a slide show of all pictures or rotate the picture right or left.

Sharing Content

Often you will want to share the documents, pictures, and other files on your computer with others. Some people might have a computer on your network at work or home, in which case you can share files with them via the network. They can then access files on the network from their own computers. Using the tools on the Share tab of File Explorer you can manage the sharing process.

Share Content with Individuals

1 With File Explorer open, click the Share tab.

2 In the Share With list, click the Specific People option.

3 Click a person's name.

4 Click Read or Read/Write to give the sharing permission you prefer.

5 Click the Share button.

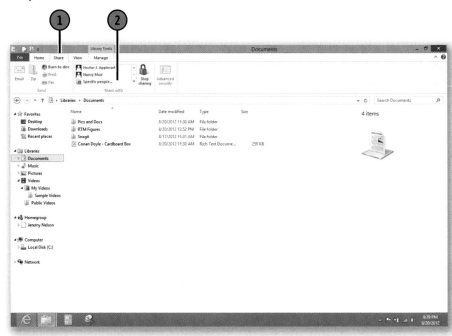

Tip

To stop sharing with a group or individual, on the File Explorer Share tab, click the group or individual on the list and then click the Stop Sharing button.

Tip

You can also use the Send group of tools on the Share tab to share content by emailing, printing, or faxing a copy of your file to another person

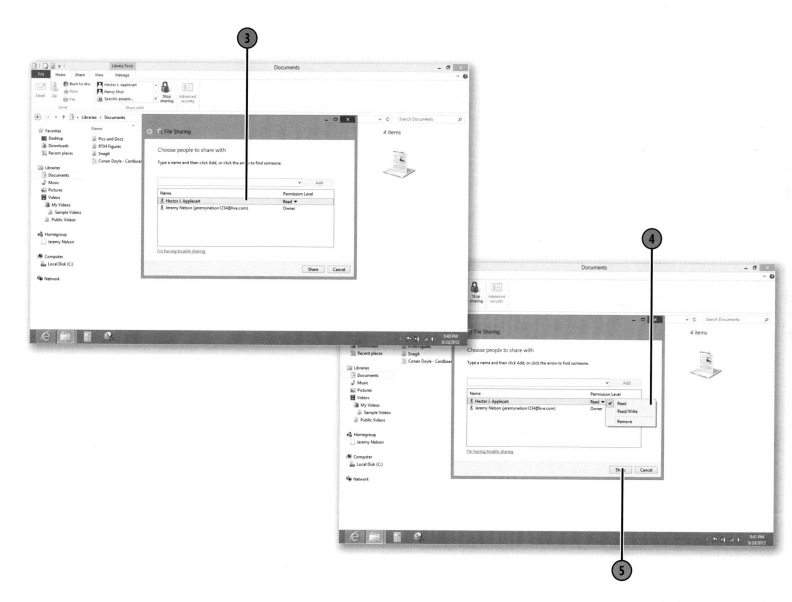

Creating Folders

The library folders in Windows 8 provide a basic set of categories for organizing files, but most people require more of a breakdown for the files they create. For example, as you create documents, you might decide to create subfolders in the Documents library for each project or client with whom you work. If you import lots of pictures into your Pictures library, you might want to break these down into folders such as Vacation, Grandkids, or Remodeling Project. The ability to create new folders and to rename files and folders is one you'll really appreciate as time goes by.

Create a New Folder

1. With File Explorer open, double-click to open the library or folder where you want to create a new folder.

2. Click the Home tab.

3. Click the New Folder button.

4. Enter a name for the folder and press Enter.

See Also

See the task "Create a New Library" earlier in this chapter if you have created folders that you want saved in a different category than those predefined in Windows 8.

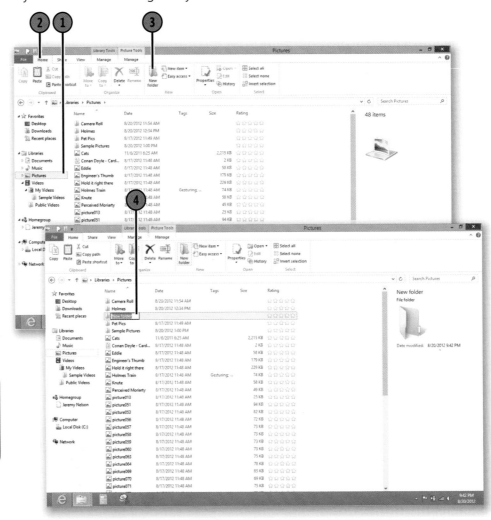

Renaming Files and Folders

Sometimes it's useful to change the name of a file or folder. For example, you might create a file called Household Budget to keep track of this year's expenses. But next year, when you create a new Household Budget file that you decide to name

2014 Budget, you might want to go back and rename Household Budget to 2013 Budget. It's simple to change the name of a file or folder to help you stay organized.

Rename a File or Folder

1. With File Explorer open, locate the file or folder you want to rename and click to select it.

2. Click the Home tab.

3. Click the Rename button.

4. Enter a new name for the file or folder and press Enter.

Tip

You cannot give two files in the same folder the same name, so when you rename a file or folder, make the new name unique. For example, if you are renumbering files named Project 1, Project 2, and Project 3 because you're about to create a new Project 1 file, you can't change Project 2 to Project 3 while another file with that name exists. In this case, you would rename Project 3 to Project 4 first; then rename 2 to 3 and 1 to 2 before adding a new Project 1.

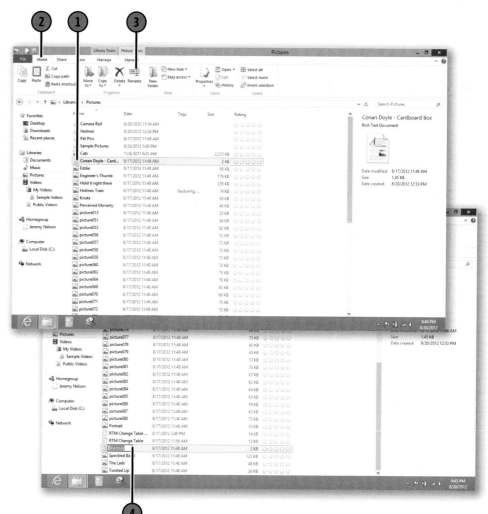

Moving and Copying Files

The way you organize files on your computer is seldom static. For example, files for this year's receipts get moved into an Old Receipts file; or you decide it would be handy to have a copy of your home inventory in both your insurance and budget folders; and so on. To deal with these changes, you need to know how to move a file from one folder to another and how to place a copy of a file in another folder. These procedures are easy to perform by using a Drag and Drop method.

Move a File to Another Folder

1. Open File Explorer.

2. Locate the file you want to move by using one of the methods in the "Finding Files and Folders with File Explorer" section, described earlier in this chapter.

3. Drag the file to another folder in the left pane of File Explorer.

4. Release your mouse button, and the file has been moved.

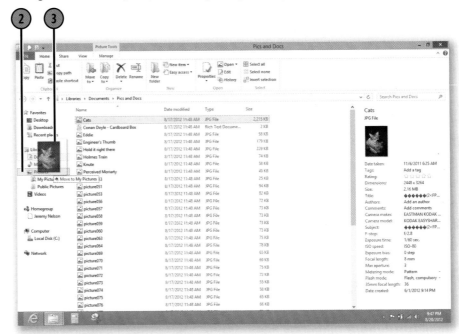

Try This!

If you want to move a file to a folder that isn't visible in the left pane—for example, to a folder on an external drive or network—after selecting the file, on the Home tab, click the Move To button, and then click Choose Location on the menu that appears. In the Move Items dialog box that is displayed, locate a drive and folder destination and then click the Move button.

Copy a File to Another Folder

① Open File Explorer.

② Use one of the methods described in the "Finding Files and Folders with File Explorer" section earlier in this chapter to locate the file you want to copy.

③ Press Ctrl and drag the file to another folder in the left pane of File Explorer.

④ Release your mouse button. The file has now been copied.

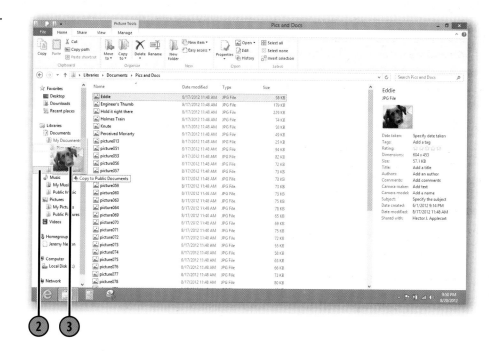

Tip

To create a copy of a file within the same folder, simply follow steps 1 and 2 above, but in step 3 drag the file to the blank area of the middle pane and it will be copied into the open folder with the word "Copy" added to the end of the file name.

Creating Compressed Files

If you want to save space on your drive or take several files and squeeze them together into a file that is smaller than the combined file sizes so that you can send them as an email attachment, you can compress the files. The compressed, or *zipped*, files you create are perfect for archiving sets of documents or sending content more quickly across the Internet. The easiest way to create a compressed file is to select files already contained in the same folder.

Create a Compressed File

1. Locate the files you want to compress by using File Explorer.

2. Click the first file.

3. Press and hold Shift and then click the last file in a sequence of adjacent files; or press and hold Ctrl and then click non-adjacent files, one by one.

4. Right-click the selected files, click Send to, and then click Compressed (Zipped) Folder.

5. Enter a name for the folder and press Enter.

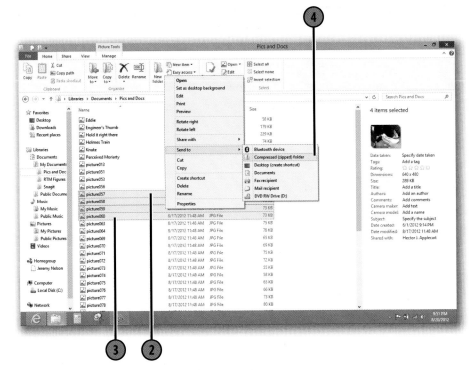

Extracting Files from a Compressed File

When you want to use the individual files in a compressed file, you can extract them back to their original, uncompressed state. When you extract files, Windows offers to create a new subfolder for the uncompressed file in the same folder where the compressed file is stored.

Extract Compressed Files

1. Locate a compressed file by using File Explorer.

2. Click the file.

3. Click the Extract tab.

4. Click the Extract All button.

5. If you want to extract the files to a folder other than the one suggested, click the Browse button and locate the folder.

6. Click Extract.

Backing Up Files

It's good practice to save your work. You can use a few methods to do this. You can turn on the File History feature, which saves libraries, your desktop settings, contacts, and favorites to a hard disk. You can also burn files to a disc by using the File Explorer Share tab.

Save Your File History

1. Insert a USB stick, or attach an external hard disk to your computer.

2. Display the desktop.

3. Press Windows logo key+X.

4. Click the Control Panel option on the menu that appears.

5. In the System And Security section, click Save Back Up Copies Of Files With File History.

6. Click the Turn On button to turn File History on.

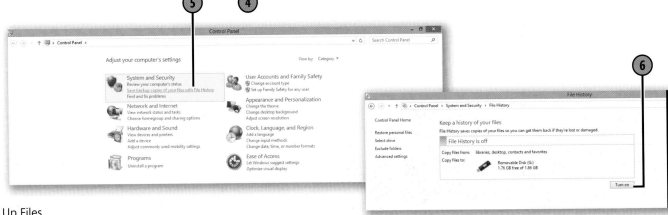

Burn Content to a Disc

1. Place a writable disc in your CD/DVD drive.

2. On the Start screen, click File Explorer.

3. Locate and select the content you want to save.

4. Click the Share tab.

5. Click the Burn To Disc button.

6. Click to select Like A USB Flash Drive or With A CD/DVD Player (as you might if you're burning a music file to the disc).

7. Click Next. Windows formats your disc and burns the file(s) to it.

Tip

You can also simply copy files to another drive by using the Copy and Paste buttons on the Home tab of File Explorer, or by clicking and dragging selected files and folders between two File Explorer windows.

See Also

See the "Copy a File to Another Folder" task earlier in this chapter for more information about copying files from one place to another.

Deleting Files and Folders

An important part of managing files on your computer is to know when to get rid of files that you no longer need. Deleting unneeded files gets rid of clutter and makes it easier to find what you want as well as frees up hard-disk space. It's a good idea to back up files before deleting (see the preceding task). However, if you delete a file and then decide you need it back,

you do have a window of time in which you can retrieve it from the Recycle Bin. (That window is determined by how much content the Recycle Bin can hold; when it fills up, older files are deleted.) This section provides the procedures both for deleting files and for retrieving files.

Delete Files

1. In File Explorer, locate the file or folder you want to delete.

2. Click the item to select it.

3. On the Home tab, click the Delete button.

Tip

If you click the Cut button instead of the Delete button, the file is moved to the Windows Clipboard. You can go to another folder in File Explorer and use the Paste button to paste the file into that location. If you don't paste the file anywhere, it will eventually disappear from the Clipboard, and you can't get it back.

Retrieve Content from the Recycle Bin

① On the desktop, double-click the Recycle Bin.

② Scroll or search to locate the file that you want to restore and then click to select it.

③ Click the Restore The Selected Items button.

④ Click the Close button.

To permanently delete files from your computer, you can use the Empty Recycle Bin button in the Recycle Bin to remove all contents. However, remember that although files might be gone from the Recycle Bin and unavailable to you, they might still be on your hard disk. If you are giving away or selling your computer, consider wiping your hard disk clean to protect your data by using software such as WipeDrive or DataEraser.

If you want to restore the entire contents of the Recycle Bin to the folders from which you deleted them, with the Recycle Bin open, click the Restore All Items button.

Sharing Settings and Files

Windows 8 provides two useful ways to connect your computing devices and content together via the Internet by using the *cloud*.

You can sync your Windows 8 device to another Windows 8–based device. This essentially shares various settings such as:

- Personalization of your desktop's ease of access features
- Access to apps you've purchased from Microsoft
- Sign-in credentials for some sites
- Some app settings

Syncing requires that the computer logs on with a Microsoft Live ID rather than using a local account. You can then sign into that Windows Live account from another Windows 8–based device, and you'll have access to these settings.

The other way that Windows 8 takes advantage of the cloud is by enabling you to share files with others by using Microsoft SkyDrive. SkyDrive lets you share items, such as pictures and documents, with others. Using SkyDrive, you can essentially make all the contents of your computer available when you log on securely from other computers.

Confirming Your Device

To sync any sign-in information for accounts or apps, you must first confirm your computer as a trusted Device.

Set Up Windows 8 to Sync

1. Press Windows logo key+I.

2. Click Change PC Settings.

3. Under Users, click Trust This PC.

4. Enter your Microsoft Live account password.

5. Click Sign In.

6. Click Confirm.

7. Verify that your email address is listed correctly on the following screen and then click the Send Link button.

8. Go to your email account and click the link in the Windows Live Account Security Confirmation email.

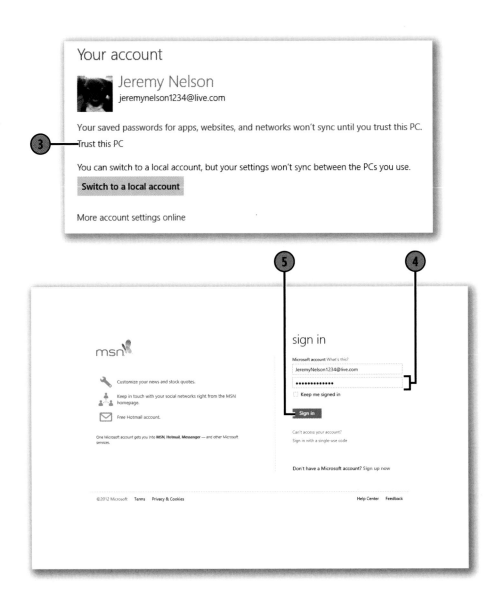

Turning on Sync

To sync, you have to turn on the sync feature. When this is turned on and you sign in to your Windows Live account on another device, your settings are synced from the cloud to that device.

Turn On the Sync Feature

1. Press Windows logo key+I.
2. Click Change PC Settings.
3. Click Sync Your Settings.
4. Click the Sync Your Settings On This PC On/Off button.

Tip

Syncing works with app settings only for apps that you've purchased from the Windows Store. See Section 14, "Buying Apps at the Windows Store," for more information about shopping for apps.

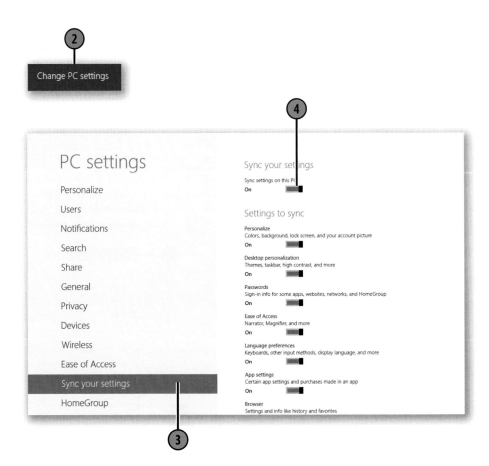

Choosing What to Sync

You don't have to share all your settings when you turn on the sync feature; you can pick and choose only the items you want to share, from language preferences to browser settings and sign-in information.

Choose Settings to Sync

1 Press Windows logo key+I.

2 Click Change PC Settings.

3 In the list of settings on the left, click Sync Your Settings.

4 Click the On/Off buttons, as preferred, for the available sync settings.

2

Change PC settings

Sync your settings

Sync settings on this PC
On

Settings to sync

Personalize
Colors, background, lock screen, and your account picture
On

Desktop personalization
Themes, taskbar, high contrast, and more
On

Passwords
Sign-in info for some apps, websites, networks, and HomeGroup
4 — On

Ease of Access
Narrator, Magnifier, and more
On

Language preferences
Keyboards, other input methods, display language, and more
On

App settings
Certain app settings and purchases made in an app
On

Tip

If you don't want items to sync when you're being charged for connection time, in the PC Settings, display Sync Settings, and then click the On/Off button under Metered Internet Connections at the bottom of the Sync Your Settings panel.

Sharing Files on Your Computer by Using SkyDrive

You can share files on your computer with SkyDrive directly from within certain apps, such as Music and Photos. This is especially useful when sending large files as email attachments is impractical. You can also open the SkyDrive app and add files to folders from there, which is covered in the "Adding Files to a Folder" task later in this chapter.

Share Your Files

1. On the Start screen, click the Photos tile.
2. Click a library.
3. Click an image.
4. Press Windows logo key+C.
5. Click Share.
6. Click Mail.
7. Click Send Using SkyDrive Instead.
8. Enter the email address associated with your SkyDrive account.
9. Click Send.
10. Open your email account.
11. Click View New Folder On SkyDrive.

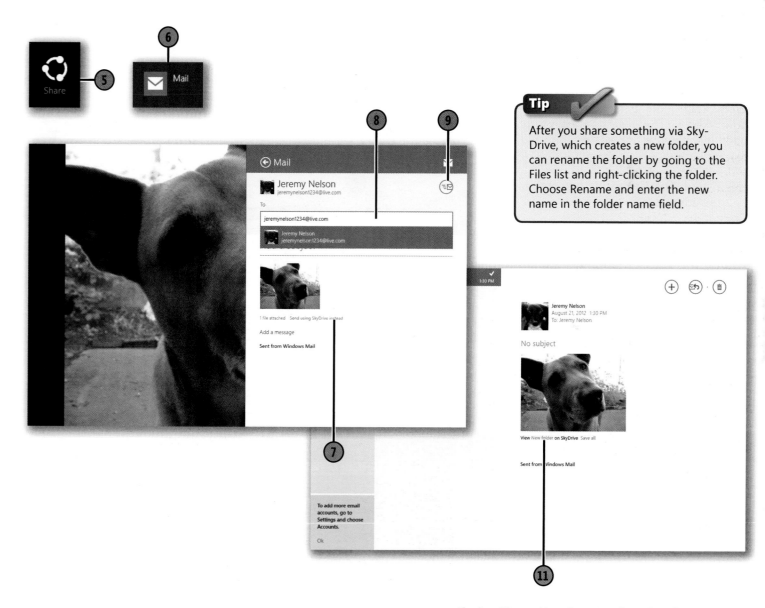

Tip

After you share something via Sky-Drive, which creates a new folder, you can rename the folder by going to the Files list and right-clicking the folder. Choose Rename and enter the new name in the folder name field.

Creating a New Folder in SkyDrive

Just as files in the libraries on your computer are organized into folders, you can organize your shared files into folders on SkyDrive. You can then share individual folders with differ- ent people so that nobody has access to your entire SkyDrive content.

Create a New Folder

1. Click the Internet Explorer tile.
2. Right-click to display the address bar.
3. Enter **https://skydrive.live.com** in the address bar.
4. Press Enter.
5. Click Create and then click Folder.
6. Enter a name for the folder.
7. Click anywhere outside of the folder to save the name.

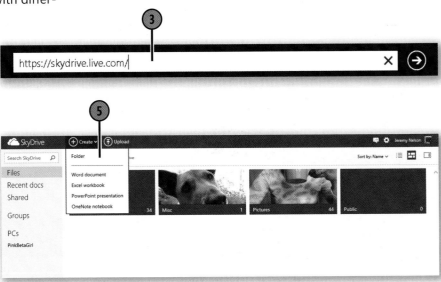

Tip

Folders in SkyDrive are displayed in columns such as the following: Name, organized alphabetically by file name; Date Modi- fied, organized by the last added or saved file; or Shared With, which identifies those that aren't shared with the words "Just me" or those that are shared with the words "Some people." To change the view from a list of files to folder/file thumbnails, use the Thumbnails View and Details View buttons to the right of the search field.

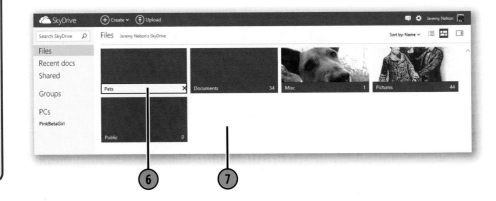

Adding Files to a Folder

After you have created a folder in SkyDrive, you can upload files to that folder. It's often easier to share larger files by adding them to SkyDrive rather than attaching them to emails.

Add Files to SkyDrive

1. Click the Internet Explorer tile.
2. Right-click to display the address bar.
3. Enter **https://skydrive.live.com** in the address bar.
4. Press Enter.
5. Click a folder to open it.
6. Click Upload.
7. Drag the scroll bar to locate the file you need. (If it's not displayed, click the Go Up button to display more folders on your computer.)
8. Click a file.
9. Click Open.

Tip

To delete a file from SkyDrive, locate it in a folder in the Files list and then right-click it. Choose Delete, and in the confirming dialog box that appears, click Yes. You can delete more than one file in a folder by selecting several check boxes in the file list and then right-clicking one of the selected files and choosing Delete.

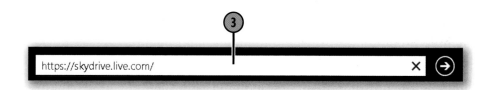

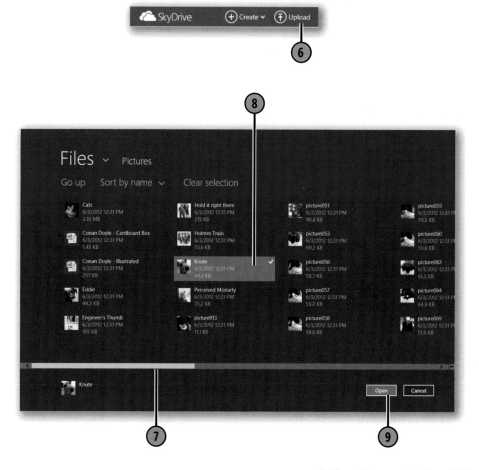

Sharing a Folder

One of the main functions of a file sharing site such as SkyDrive is, quite logically, to share content with others. You can share individual folders of content and allow people to edit the content or only read it.

Share a Folder

1. With SkyDrive open, click Files to display the Files list.

2. Right-click a folder.

3. Choose Share.

4. Enter an email address.

5. Enter a note (optional).

6. If you don't want the person to edit files, clear the Recipients Can Edit check box.

7. Click Share.

Tip

Instead of sending a notification email, you can send a link to the SkyDrive folder that allows people to only view files, view and edit, or make the folder viewable by anybody. Click the Get A Link button in the dialog box shown in the second figure on this page to create these links.

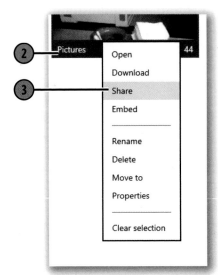

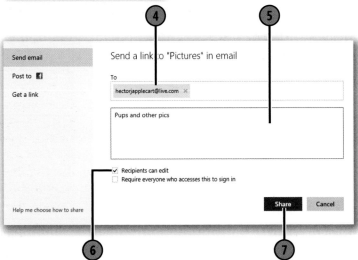

Going Online with Internet Explorer 10

In this section:

- **Exploring Internet Explorer 10**
- **Navigating Among Websites**
- **Searching on a Page**
- **Searching with Bing**
- **Creating Tabs**
- **Using Pinned and Frequently Visited Sites**
- **Overview of the Internet Explorer Desktop**

Internet Explorer is Microsoft's web browser. You use a browser to navigate around the Internet, the worldwide network of computers that contains the content that makes up the World Wide Web. In addition to helping you move among websites and display web content, a browser helps you to stay organized by displaying several open websites on tabs and helping you to find specific content on pages.

Windows 8 includes a tile on the Start screen for Internet Explorer 10. IE 10, as it's often called, is optimized for the Windows 8 interface, including the ability to use it with a touchscreen computing device. The main paradigm for Windows 8 and Internet Explorer 10 is to show as much content as possible on the screen at any time, rather than cluttering up the screen with toolbars and menus. The browser is easy to navigate and simple to use, after you get the hang of it.

In this section, you discover the various features of Internet Explorer 10 and get an overview of the Internet Explorer 10 browser that appears if you open it from the Windows 8 desktop.

Exploring Internet Explorer 10

In Internet Explorer 10, one big difference from previous versions of Internet Explorer is that there are no tools on the screen until you display them. For example, you have to display the address bar to use it. The address bar is a stalwart of browsers. You use this field to enter a website address, such as www.microsoft.com, to go to that page. However, starting with Internet Explorer 9, that field has a dual purpose. You can still enter a URL, but you can also use the field to search the web for content and sites.

Open Internet Explorer 10

① Press the Windows logo key on your keyboard.

② Click the Internet Explorer tile.

Tip If you open Internet Explorer from the Start screen you go to a different version of Internet Explorer than you do if you click the IE button on the desktop taskbar.

Use the Address Bar

① With Internet Explorer 10 open, on the Start screen, right-click the screen.

② Click the address bar, and begin to type a URL, such as **www.bing.com** or **http://www.amazon.com**.

③ Press Enter to go to the address.

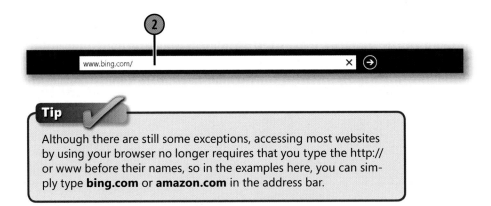

Tip Although there are still some exceptions, accessing most websites by using your browser no longer requires that you type the http:// or www before their names, so in the examples here, you can simply type **bing.com** or **amazon.com** in the address bar.

Navigating Among Websites

When you are browsing the Internet, you will want to move from one website or webpage to another. You can do this in several ways: you can enter a URL in the address bar as covered in the previous task; move backward or forward to a previ- ously visited site; or click a hyperlink (text or an image that is programmed to send you to another location on the Internet when you click it).

Move Among Websites

① Open Internet Explorer 10 from the Start screen, and move your mouse to the left side of the screen and click the Back button to go to the previously viewed site.

② Move your mouse to the right side of the screen, and click the Forward button to go to the website on which you started.

Follow Links

① With a webpage displayed (use http:// windows.microsoft.com, for example), click a graphic or text link to follow a link.

② Click a link on the subsequent page to follow it.

③ To return to the page from which you fol- lowed the link, move your mouse cursor to the left side of the screen.

④ Click the Back button.

Tip

On some sites, if you right-click or select text and right-click, a message will display, warning you that the site is copyrighted, or you might see tools such as the copy command displayed.

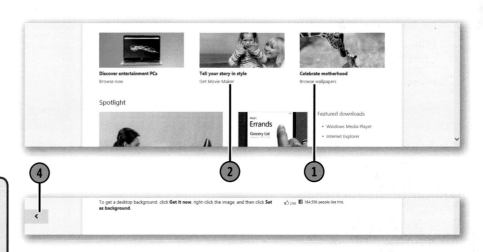

Tip

Text links are colored, often (but not always) in blue to help you spot them. After you follow a link, if you return to the page it was displayed on, the link will usually appear in purple rather than blue, indicating that it's been clicked at least once.

Searching on a Page

Individual webpages on a website can be quite long. You can use scroll bars in your browser to move down a page, or you can search to find specific contents on a page. In Internet Explorer 10, you can use a Find On Page feature to search for and scroll through all highlighted instances of a search term on the currently active page.

Search for Content on a Page

1. Navigate to the page you want to search.

2. Right-click.

3. Click the Page Tools button.

4. Click Find On Page.

5. Enter a word or phrase.

6. Click the Previous or Next button.

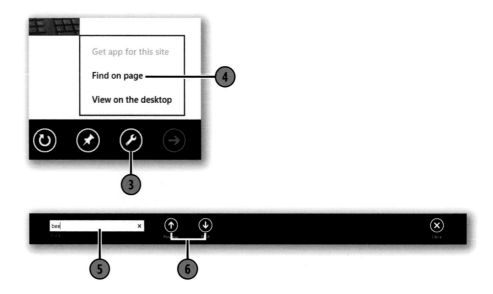

Tip

When you enter a search term, such as "win," your results will include all words that contain those letters, such as Windows and winner. To narrow your search to only the word "win" in this example, simply enclose the term with quotation marks.

Tip

Use the Get App For This Site selection from the Page Tools button menu to download any associated app for sites such as *Zune.com* or *Amazon.com*.

Searching with Bing

There's a lot of content on the Internet, and using your browser to find what you need is an important skill that you should master. If you want to search the entire web for a site, page, or document, you can do so in Internet Explorer 10 by typing a search term in the address bar or by using a search engine such as Bing or Google. You can go to a particular search engine by entering its URL, such as www.bing.com, in the address bar and pressing Enter. Bing is the default search engine if you use the address bar to search.

Search the Internet

(1) With Internet Explorer 10 open, right-click the screen.

(2) Enter a search term, such as **pollution**, in the address bar.

(3) Press Enter.

(4) Click in the Bing search field.

(5) To narrow your search further, enter a search term such as **water pollution**.

(6) Click Search.

(7) Click a category such as Images or News to narrow your search.

(8) Click any result to go to that site.

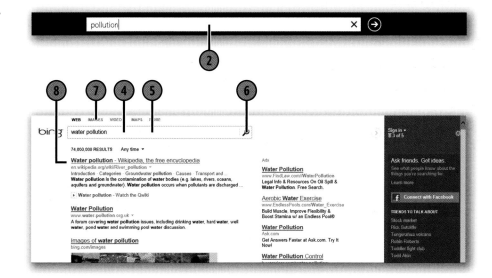

Tip

If you want to make changes to Bing search settings, click the Preferences button in the upper-right corner. In the page that appears, you can filter adult content, turn on Search Suggestions, change the display language, and specify your location so that results are more relevant to you.

Creating Tabs

Tabbed browsing is a feature of some browsers that allows you to have several sites open at once so that you can move back and forth among them with a click. In Internet Explorer 10, the tab feature has been reinvented. Tabs aren't displayed onscreen taking up screen real estate; instead, you can display tabs by right-clicking the screen and then click a tab to go to a site, or add and close tabs.

Create New Tabs

1. Open Internet Explorer from the Start screen.

2. Right-click.

3. Click the Add Tab button.

4. Click a Frequent or Favorite item, or enter the URL of a site.

5. If necessary, click the site you want to add from the results.

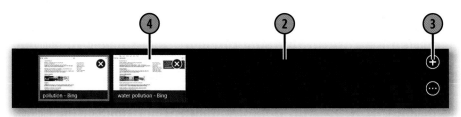

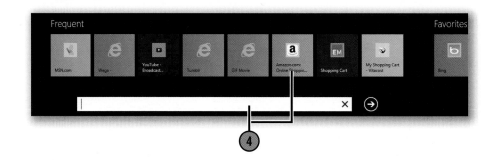

Tip

To open a link on a new tab, instead of clicking the link, right-click it and choose the Open Link In New Tab command.

Using Pinned and Frequently Visited Sites

You can pin a site to your Start screen so that you can get to it quickly. For example, if you use a search engine regularly or if you use a cloud player to play your music selections, you might want to be able to access that site on your Start screen. After it's pinned, you can click the tile for that site and go to it instantly by using Internet Explorer 10.

Pin a Site

1 Go to the site you want to pin to the Start screen.

2 Right-click.

3 Click the Page Tools button.

4 Click View On The Desktop.

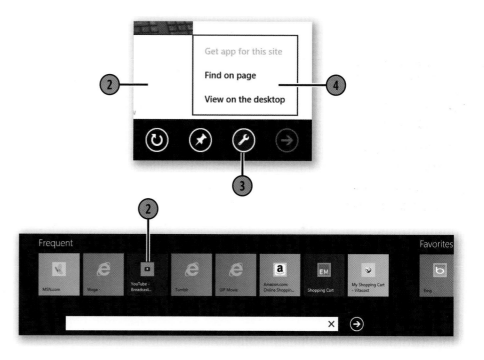

Visit Frequent Sites

1 Press Alt+D.

2 Click an item in the Frequent category to go there.

Tip

To remove a frequent site, press Alt+D to display the Frequent sites, right-click a site, and then click Remove.

Overview of the Internet Explorer Desktop App

When you display Internet Explorer 10 from the desktop, you see a more traditional browser window with an address bar, tabs, and the ability to display additional toolbars. To display additional toolbars, right-click the top of the screen and click to display the Favorites, Menu, and Command bars to see the tools shown here. If you've used recent versions of Internet Explorer, many of these features might be familiar to you.

Print menu

Safety Menu

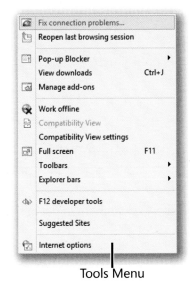

Tools Menu

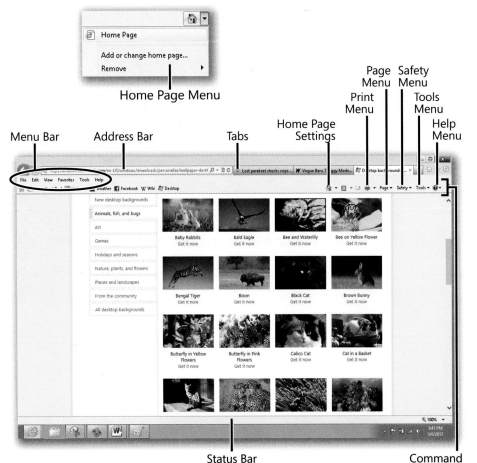

Home Page Menu

Menu Bar

Address Bar

Tabs

Home Page Settings

Page Menu

Safety Menu

Print Menu

Tools Menu

Help Menu

Status Bar

Command Bar Tools

Help Menu

13

Using Mail and Messaging

Email is an important way to stay connected for a great many people. Microsoft offers its Windows Live Hotmail accounts for free. In this section, you learn how to set up an email account and then how to use Hotmail tools to read, reply to, and forward messages. You explore organizing messages in folders and working with message attachments.

In addition, this section introduces you to the Messaging app. Using this app, you can receive and send instant messages to another's telephone number or email account. Instant messaging or IM is a more immediate communication tool than email because you typically connect with people in real time, rather than experiencing the delay that happens when people don't pick up and respond to email right away.

Setting Up an Email Account

You can set up accounts for most email providers and access one or more of those accounts by using the Mail app. For major providers such as Hotmail and Google, the process is typically simple to do.

Set Up an Email Account

1. Click the Mail tile.

2. Press Windows logo key+I.

3. Click Accounts.

4. Click Add An Account.

5. Click Hotmail, Outlook, Google, or Other Account.

6. Enter an email address.

7. Enter the password.

8. If adding a Google account, click the Include your Google Contacts and Calendars checkbox if you want to access these features from Mail.

9. Click Connect.

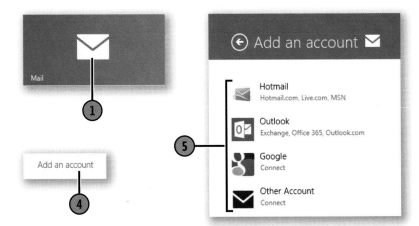

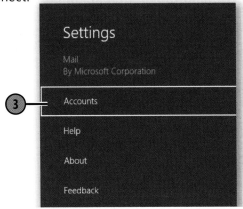

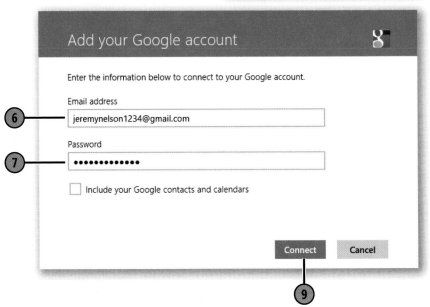

Opening Mail in Hotmail

To help you learn the ins and outs of using email, you can explore Hotmail. (You might already have a Windows Live account that you can use for this.) As with all email services, your incoming mail appears in an Inbox folder.

Check Your Inbox

1 On the Start screen, click the Mail tile.

2 Click the email account you want to use, if you have set up more than one.

3 Click Inbox.

Tip

Note that each message in your Inbox indicates the date it was received. Some also display a small paperclip icon indicating the message includes an attachment.

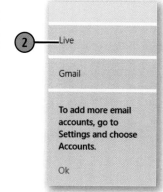

Reading and Replying to Messages

After you open your Inbox, you will want to read messages and, in some cases, reply to them. You can reply to just the sender or to others to whom the message was addressed.

Read a Message

1. On the Start screen, click the Mail tile.

2. Click the email account you want to check, if you've set up more than one account.

3. Click a message and read it.

The Mail app displays Inbox folders, messages, and the contents of the selected message in three panels. Use the individual scroll bars in each panel to view more contents.

Reply to a Message

1. With the message displayed, click the Respond button.

2. Click Reply or Reply All.

3. Enter any additional addressees.

4. Enter your message.

5. Click Send.

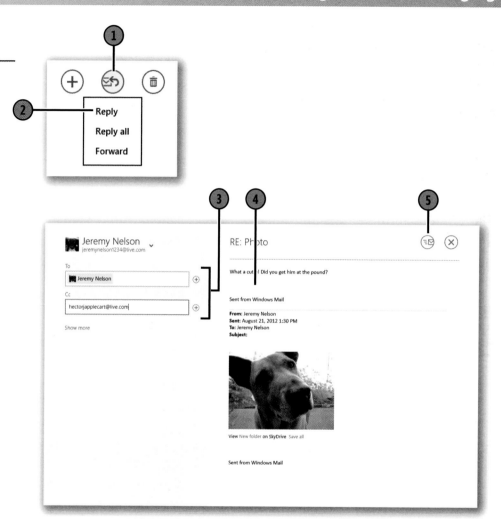

Moving Messages to Folders

If you left all the messages you receive in your Inbox, it would get very cluttered. It's better to move messages into folders, just as you organize your computer documents in folders by topic or project. Note that to delete or create new folders, you should go to your email account by using your browser and use the tools in the email program to do so.

Move a Message to a Folder

1. With the message open, right-click the screen.
2. Click Move.
3. Click the folder to which you want to move the message.

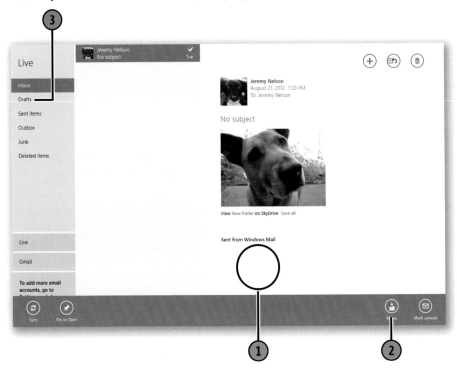

Forwarding a Message

Often when you receive a message, you will want to send it on to another person by using a process called *forwarding*. Forwarding simply involves choosing the Forward option, entering one or more email addresses, and sending the message on. You can add an additional message to the original message when you forward.

Forward a Message

1 With a message open, click Respond.

2 Click Forward.

3 Enter an address.

4 Enter a message.

5 Click Send.

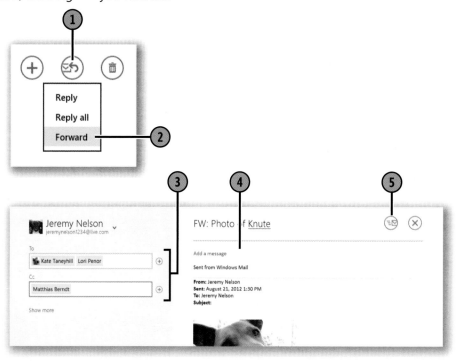

Opening Attachments

You can attach documents in various formats to an email, as well as pictures and even audio and video files. When you receive an email with an attachment, you might have choices about opening the attachment online, downloading it, or saving it with its original or a new name to a preferred location on your hard drive or an external drive.

Open and Read an Attachment

1. With a message containing an attachment open, click the attachment to download it and then right-click the attachment.

2. Click Open.

3. Click and drag to scroll through the document.

4. Click Save to save the attachment.

Tip

In step 2 of this procedure, click Open With if you want to designate a non-default app to use to open the attachment. Click Save if you want to save the attached document to a folder on your hard drive or external storage.

Creating and Sending a Message

To create your own messages, open a blank email form and enter information such as the email address or addresses that you want to send the message to, anybody you want to copy on the message, the subject, and the message itself.

Create and Send a Message

1. Click the Mail tile.

2. Click the inbox of the email account you want to use.

3. Click New.

4. Enter an address or addresses.

5. Enter any addresses you want to copy on the message.

6. Enter a message.

7. Click Send.

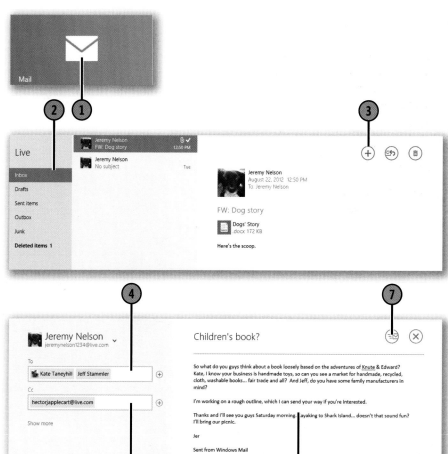

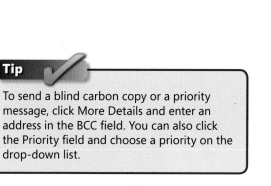

Tip

To send a blind carbon copy or a priority message, click More Details and enter an address in the BCC field. You can also click the Priority field and choose a priority on the drop-down list.

Adding Attachments

Before you send a message you've created, you might want to add an attachment to it. This is a good way to share the contents of documents or images with others. The file you want to attach must be available on your hard disk or on an external drive such as a USB flash drive.

Add an Attachment to a Message

1. With Mail open, click the New button.

2. Enter an address.

3. Right-click, and then click Attachments.

4. Click Go Up if you need to view contents of another folder or library.

5. Click a file.

6. Click Attach.

7. Enter a message.

8. Click Send.

> **Tip**
>
> Email accounts typically have a limit for the size of attachments that can be sent through the account. If you have to share very large files, consider using the Windows 8 feature that allows you to compress several files into one file of a smaller size before attaching (see Section 10, "File Management") or sharing your files—for example, when using an online service such as SkyDrive, discussed in Section 11, "Sharing Settings and Files."

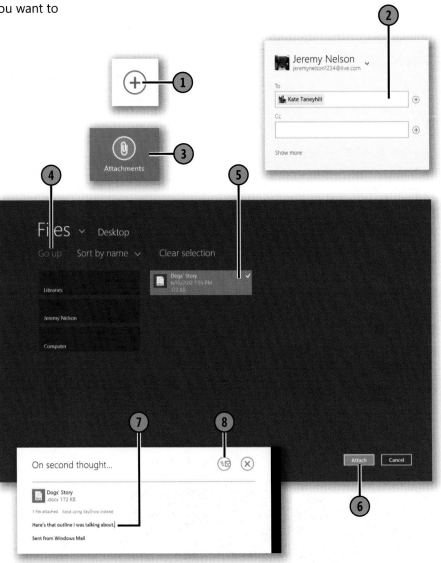

Reading and Replying to Instant Messages

The Messaging app available on the Windows 8 Start screen allows you to tap into the power of instant messaging, where you can hold a real-time text conversation with another person via their email address or phone number.

Read and Reply to Messages

1 Click the Messaging tile on the Start screen.

2 Click a thread.

3 Read any displayed messages.

4 Click in the messaging text box, and enter a message.

5 Press Enter.

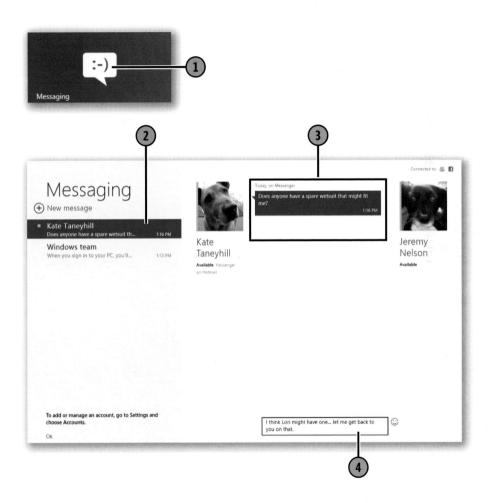

Adding a Friend

You can invite friends to exchange messages with you. When you add somebody as a friend in the Messaging app, you are inviting that person to send you messages.

Invite a Friend

1. Click the Messaging app on the Start screen.

2. Right-click.

3. Click Invite.

4. Click Add A Friend. If Messaging requests privacy information, enter it.

5. Enter a name or email address.

6. Click Next.

7. Click Invite.

Tip

In step 5, you can also click the Select From Your Contact List link or the Search For People link to find people if you don't know their email address.

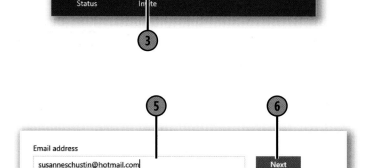

Email address

susanneschustin@hotmail.com

Next

Add people to your contacts list from networks like Facebook, LinkedIn, Twitter and others

Invite

Deleting a Thread

When you have carried on an instant messaging conversation with one or more people, you might want to delete the thread that contains all those messages to remove clutter from your screen.

Delete a Thread

(1) Click the Messaging tile on the Start screen.

(2) Click a message thread.

(3) Right-click.

(4) Click Delete.

(5) Click Delete to delete the conversation.

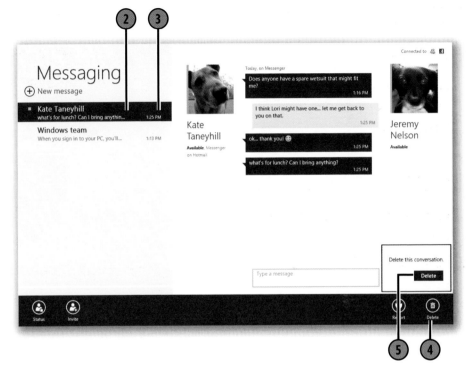

Changing Your Online Status

When you use instant messaging, you let people who are your friends know when you are available and when you're offline. If you're online but busy, you might choose to change your status to invisible so that, to the world, you appear as offline and unavailable.

Let People Know Whether You're Available

1. Click the Messaging tile on the Start screen.

2. Right-click.

3. Click Status.

4. Click Available or Invisible.

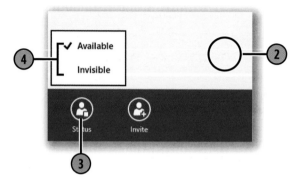

Buying Apps at the Windows Store

The Windows Store is a collection of free and paid apps that open up a world of computing activities. If you want to dabble in painting on your computer, you might buy an inexpensive app instead of more robust design software. Need an app to help you find your way around Italy on your next vacation? There's an app for that. And if you love games, you'll love all the game apps in the Windows Store.

In this section, you discover how to find the app you need, either by using the integrated search feature of Windows 8 or by browsing different categories in the Windows Store itself. After you know how to find the apps you want, you can download free apps and buy paid apps. You can also discover how to find app reviews to make sure you're getting the best app for you, and to add your own app ratings and reviews to help others find their way.

Get ready to explore apps, a whole new dynamic for acquiring functionality for your Windows-based computing device.

Searching for Apps

The first way to find an app is by searching for it. When you use the Windows 8 search feature, you can select from various locations to search, including the Windows Store. When you click an app in the search results, you're directed to the Windows Store.

Find an App

① On the Start screen, begin typing an app name such as **cooking**.

② Click Store.

③ Click All Categories to choose an app category.

④ Click All Prices to view Paid and Free apps.

⑤ Click Sort By Relevance to choose a sort criterion.

⑥ Click an app to open details in the Windows Store.

Try This!

To find the most popular apps, use the steps in this procedure to search for an app by entering a word such as **weather**, and then use the Sort By Relevance list and choose Sort by Highest Rating as your sort criterion.

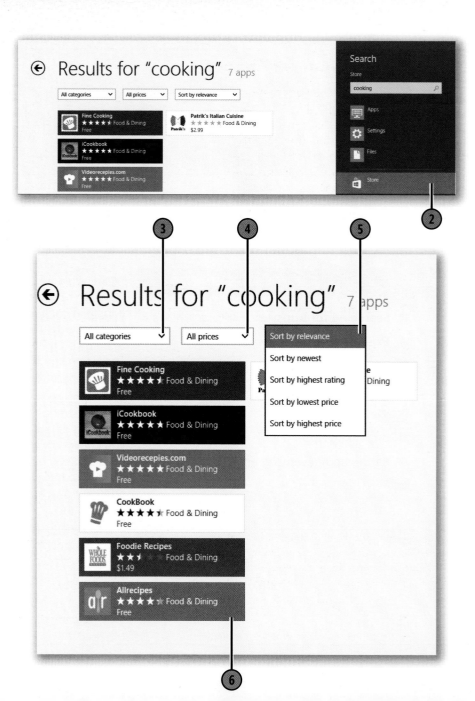

Exploring the Windows Store

The Windows Store offers a very easy-to-navigate interface with graphical ties for available apps, all organized into categories such as Games, Social, Education, Health & Fitness, and Entertainment. Use these categories to browse available apps and see featured free or paid apps.

Explore the Windows Store

① Click the Store tile.

② In the lower-right of the window, click the right arrow of the scroll bar to move through the categories.

③ Click a feature such as Top Free or New Releases.

④ Click an app to display details about it.

⑤ Click the Back button to go back to the Store home screen.

Tip

The Spotlight category includes new or interesting apps that you might want to check out. Exploring the apps in this category helps you keep up with the latest, greatest apps.

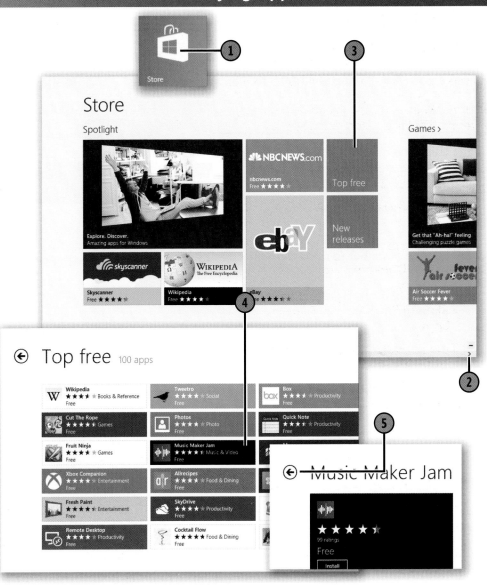

Reading App Reviews

Before you buy any app, it's a good idea to see what other people think of it. Even though some apps are free and paid apps aren't typically as expensive as desktop software such as Microsoft Office, you still want to make the best choice you can for your needs, saving yourself time and money by getting the right app, right from the start.

Read Reviews

① Using the methods in the previous tasks, locate an app you're interested in.

② Click the app to display details.

③ Click Reviews.

④ Use the scroll bar to scroll through the reviews.

⑤ Click the Sort By field to display sort options.

Tip

When you view the details of an app in the Windows Store, you can use the app website link to visit the app producer's site, where you might find more useful reviews to read before you buy.

Installing Free Apps

There's nothing better than free, and the Windows Store offers quite a few free apps to explore. When you get a free app, you simply click an Install button and the app downloads to your computer.

Get a Free App

① Locate an app by using either of the methods in the first two tasks of this section.

② Click the app to display details.

③ Click Install.

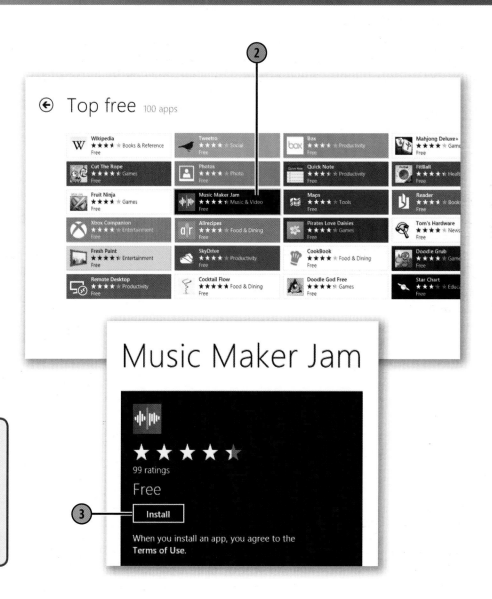

Apps you download from the Store are pinned to the Start screen; you can open an app by clicking its tile. To unpin an app on the Start screen, in the toolbar that appears, right-click the app tile and then click Unpin From Start. You can then open the app by typing its name on the Start screen, and then in the results area, click the app.

Viewing Your Apps

You can view all the apps you've purchased in the store along with some tools for sorting the apps. Note that you can view any apps you've purchased, whether you downloaded them to the device you're using or to another Windows 8–based device if you're logged in with the same Windows Live account.

See the Apps You Own

1. Click the Store tile.
2. Right-click.
3. Click Your Apps.
4. Click to choose to view all apps purchased or only those installed on the current computer.
5. Click to sort apps by date or name.

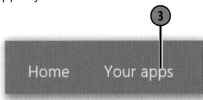

Tip

As long as you sign into your Microsoft Live account on any of your Windows 8–based devices, you will see all the apps you've purchased, from any of your devices.

Buying an App

When you find an app you'd like to make your own, you can follow a typical purchase procedure to enter payment information and submit your order.

Buy Apps

1. Locate an app in the Store and click on it.
2. Click Buy.
3. Click Confirm.
4. Enter your Microsoft account password.
5. Click OK.
6. Enter payment information including your billing address.
7. Click Submit.

Tip ✓

After you've acquired some apps, when you go to the Windows Store, you'll find that updates for your apps are occasionally listed there as well. Click the Updates link, click the app updates you want to get, and then click Install.

⊖ Games 18 apps

All subcategories ⌄   Paid ⌄   Sort by noteworthy ⌄

Surly Sudoku
★★★★☆
$4.99

Doodle Grub
★★★★☆
$2.99

Oscar's adventures
★★★★☆
$1.49

Submit

Buy

Confirm

Enter your Microsoft account password

Jeremy Nelson
JeremyNelson1234@live.com

••••••••••••

Can't access your account?

OK   Cancel

⊖ Payment and billing

Choose a payment method

New payment method

⦿ Credit card

○ PayPal

Credit card

○ Visa x2308

Add payment information

Credit card type *

⦿ VISA ○ [MasterCard] ○ [AMERICAN EXPRESS] ○ [DISCOVER]

Credit card number *

Expiration date *

06 ⌄   2018 ⌄

Name on card *

Jeremy Nelson

Rating and Reviewing an App

Just as you benefit from others' reviews of an app before you invest your time and money in it, other people can benefit from your reviews. You can post a rating for any app you download from the Windows Store: a one-star rating is low, and a five-star rating is high. You can also submit a review of up to 500 characters to let others know how you liked the app.

Rate and Review an App

1. With an app open, press Windows logo key+I.

2. Click Rate and Review.

3. Click the star rating.

4. Enter a title.

5. Enter your review.

6. Click Submit.

Tip

Your reviews have to comply with Windows Store guidelines, or they can be removed. If you spot a review that's in some way offensive or not in compliance with the rules, you can click the Report This Review link on the review to report the item to Microsoft.

Settings

Fresh Paint
By Microsoft Corporation

Send feedback

Privacy Statement

Permissions

Rate and review

Notifications   Power   Unavailable

Change PC settings

Write a review or Fresh Paint

Your rating (required)

★ ★ ★ ★ ★

Title

So much fun!

Review (189/500 characters)

You can really crank out some beautiful works of art in this app. Lots of tools, surfaces, paints and pencils. Plus a handy "undo" button that can erase those last few poorly-placed lines.

Note: The name and picture for the Microsoft account you use with the Store will be posted with your review.

Submit   Cancel

15

Managing People and Time

In your busy life, you have a lot to juggle. You need to stay in touch with people, schedule appointments, and check the weather to plan your travels.

To keep track of and communicate with contacts, Windows 8 provides the People app. After you enter information about somebody in the People app, you can send her messages by using the Messaging app, email, or Facebook, and you can map that person's location by using Bing Maps.

You can use the Calendar app to create events and set reminders for those events if you like. You can also send invitations to any event by using email from within the Calendar app.

If you want to check out the weather today or on the day of an upcoming event, use the Weather app to see regional, national, and even international data about precipitation, temperature, and more.

Adding a New Contact

The People app helps you manage your contacts. You can enter information about a person, including name, company, email, phone, address, job title, significant other, and website. There is also a Notes field to add information such as birthday, favorite movie, or whatever you want to remember about that person.

After you add a contact, you can use the People app to send instant messages, post a message to that person's Facebook account, or send email. You can also map the person's location by using Bing Maps.

Add a Contact

① On the Start screen, click the People app tile.

② Right-click.

③ Click New.

④ Enter contact information in fields, such as name.

⑤ Click Save.

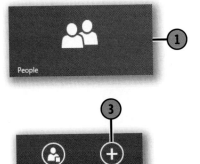

Try This!

When entering contact information, click the + symbol at the bottom of the Name field. In the menu that appears, click a choice to enter a Phonetic First Name or Phonetic Last Name so that you can remember how to pronounce an unusual name. Click Middle Name or Nickname to enter additional name information. Click Title or Suffix to add a title such as vice-president or a suffix such as Junior or Senior to a contact record.

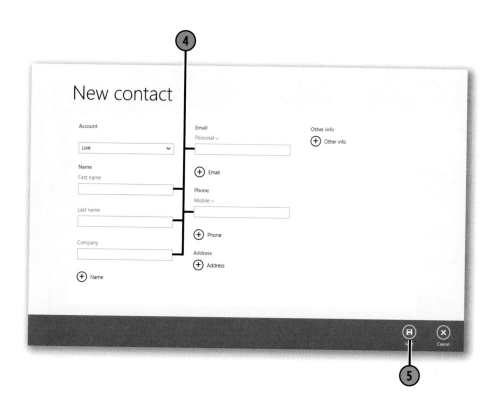

New contact

Account

Live

Name

First name

Last name

Company

⊕ Name

Email

Personal ⌄

⊕ Email

Phone

Mobile ⌄

⊕ Phone

Address

⊕ Address

Other info

⊕ Other info

Save   Cancel

Editing Contact Information

We all move, change jobs, and even change our phone numbers now and then. After you enter a contact, you might want to add more details or change information. For example, you might want to enter a new phone number or email address. You can easily make such changes and save them.

Edit Contact Details

1. On the Start screen, click the People app tile.

2. Click a contact name.

3. Right-click.

4. Click Edit.

5. Click a field.

6. Edit the entry or replace it with new text.

7. Click in an empty field, and add new information.

8. Click Save.

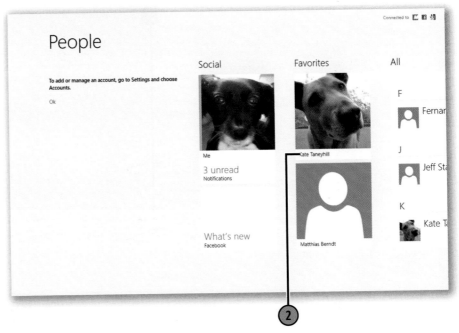

Tip

If you have entered an address for your contact, you can use the Maps app to map that address. When you open the contact information, just click Map and the location is displayed in Bing Maps. This feature requires that you have an Internet connection.

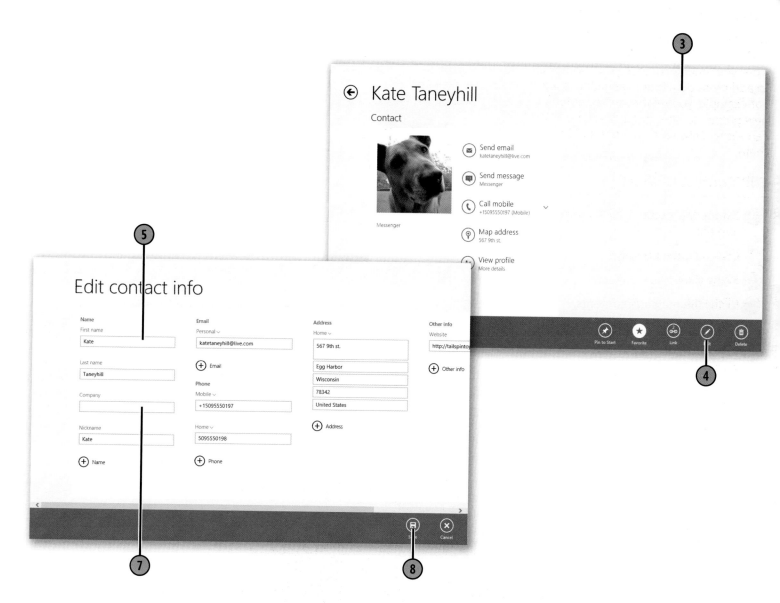

Kate Taneyhill

Contact

Send email
katetaneyhill@live.com

Send message
Messenger

Call mobile
+15095550197 (Mobile)

Map address
567 9th st.

View profile
More details

Messenger

Pin to Start   Favorite   Link   Delete

Edit contact info

Name
First name
Kate

Last name
Taneyhill

Company

Nickname
Kate

⊕ Name

Email
Personal ⌄
katetaneyhill@live.com

⊕ Email

Phone
Mobile ⌄
+15095550197

Home ⌄
5095550198

⊕ Phone

Address
Home ⌄
567 9th st.

Egg Harbor

Wisconsin

78342

United States

⊕ Address

Other info
Website
http://tailspintoy

⊕ Other info

Save   Cancel

Sending Messages to People

You can send messages to your contacts by using the People app. To do this, you must first enter an email address for the contact and be connected to the Internet. You can choose to use the Mail app, Microsoft Outlook, or an alternative mail app to send your message. For example, if you choose the Mail app, that app opens with a new email form already addressed to the contact.

Send an Email Message to a Contact

1. With the People app open and All Contacts displayed, click a contact.

2. Click Send Email.

3. If prompted, click an email app to use to send your message.

4. Enter a message subject.

5. Enter the message contents.

6. Click Send.

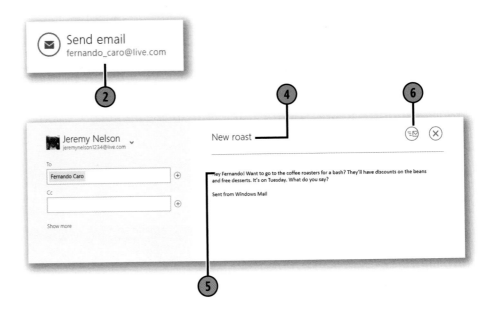

Send email
fernando_caro@live.com

Jeremy Nelson
jeremynelson1234@live.com

To
Fernando Caro

Cc

Show more

New roast

Hey Fernando! Want to go to the coffee roasters for a bash? They'll have discounts on the beans and free desserts. It's on Tuesday. What do you say?

Sent from Windows Mail

Tip

The contacts you have stored in the People app are available to other apps. For example, if you use the Mail app to send an email message, when you begin to type an addressee's name in the To field, a list of matching contacts from the People app appears. Click one to easily and quickly fill in the To field.

Setting Up Online Accounts

When you connect your Microsoft Live account to Windows 8 and have an Internet connection, you can connect to various online accounts by using the People app. For example, you can connect to Facebook, Twitter, Google, and LinkedIn. With an account connected, you can then apply settings for how to share your information and how to view information from that account. (See Section 2, "Meet the Windows 8 Interface," for more information about connecting with a Windows Live account).

Set Up Accounts

1. Display the People app with All Contacts showing.

2. Click the Microsoft Live button.

3. Click Add An Account.

4. Click an account type.

5. Provide user information, and log in according to the instructions for the type of account you've selected.

6. Click the icon to connect to the account.

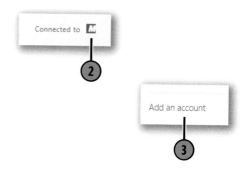

Apply Account Settings

1. With All Contacts displayed, click an account icon, such as Facebook.

2. Click the account name in the list that appears.

3. Click Manage This Account Online.

4. Enter your Windows Live password if required.

5. Click select settings.

6. Click Save.

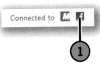

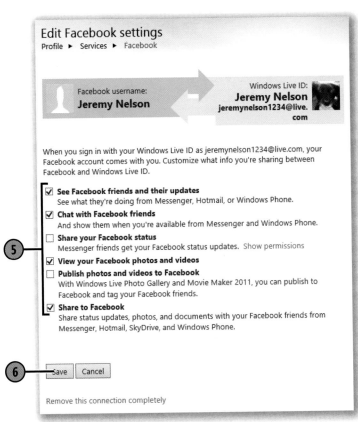

Tip

After you have set up an account on the All Contacts screen of the People app, you will see that account's logo, such as the Facebook or Twitter logo, in the upper-right corner, showing you which accounts you are connected to. If a contact has an account on a service that you're connected to, display that person's information and click the Send Message link for the appropriate service. If that person is online, you can then enter and send a message to him at that account.

Pinning Contacts to the Start Screen

If you are in touch with somebody frequently, consider pinning that contact to the Start screen. After you do that, you can simply click that person's tile to open her contact information. From that screen, you can quickly view more information about the person or send an email.

Pin a Contact to the Start Screen

1. On the Start screen, click the People app.

2. Click a contact name.

3. Right-click the next screen to display a toolbar.

4. Click Pin To Start.

5. Enter the item to pin (for example, the contact name or the contact's website).

6. Click Pin To Start.

Tip ✓

In addition to sending email from the People app, you can also download an app with which you can click a contact's phone number and call that person directly from your computer. It's best to have a headphone attached to your computer to make such Internet calls.

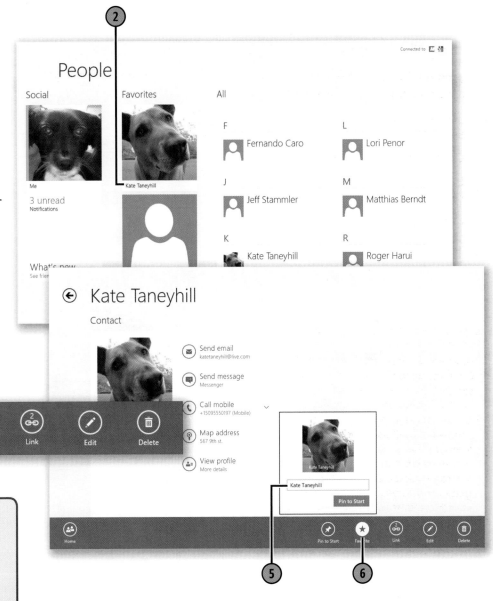

Displaying Calendar Views

Sometimes it's helpful to get different perspectives on your schedule. That's why the Calendar app offers you three views of your events: by Day, Week, or Month. From any view, you can quickly return to the Day, Week, or Month view that includes today's date. For example, if you have scrolled six months forward to enter dates for your summer vacation, you can quickly return to today's date in the current view by clicking Today.

Choose a Calendar View

1. On the Start screen, click the Calendar app.

2. Right-click the Calendar app.

3. Click Day, Week, or Month.

4. Click Today to return to today's date.

Try This!

Create a task and choose to save it to your calendar or to the Birthday or Holiday calendar. In all of the views, to help you differentiate them, events saved to My Calendar appear in green, events saved to the Birthday calendar display in a dark purple, and events saved to the Holiday calendar appear in orange.

Adding a Calendar Event

Using the Calendar app, you can create events such as appointments, vacation time, concerts or any other point in time that you want to keep a record of. You can enter many details about the event, such as where and when it will take place, how long it will run, and whether it's a recurring event.

Create an Event

① On the Start screen, click the Calendar app.

② Click a date. (In Week or Day view, click a time slot.)

③ Enter a title and description of the event.

④ Enter appropriate information for the Where, When, Start time, and How Long settings.

⑤ Click the Save this Event button.

Tip

If you want an event such as a birthday or monthly meeting to recur on a regular basis, such as every week or every year, use the How Often setting in the event's Details page. Just click the field and then click a time period: day, weekday, week, month, or year. The event is created for all recurring dates.

Tip

You need to enter only the start time and how long the event will last. The Calendar app automatically calculates the end time based on that information.

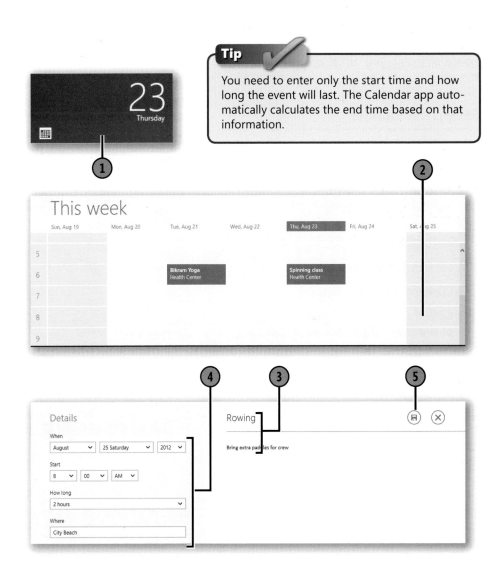

Using Reminders

One reason to enter events in the Calendar app is so that you can be reminded of those events ahead of time. When you create an event, you can also apply a setting so that you are alerted prior to the event—for example, 15 or 30 minutes ahead of the event, a day ahead, and so on. When that specified reminder time arrives, the Calendar app will send you an email about the event.

Set Up a Reminder

1. On the Start screen, click the Calendar app.

2. Click an existing event or right-click the screen and then click New.

3. If you're creating a new event, enter a start time.

4. Click the Show More link.

5. Click the Reminder field.

6. Click the setting for how far ahead of the event start time you'd like to receive a reminder.

7. Click the Save this Event button.

Tip

Sometimes it's useful to be reminded of an event a week ahead and then again a day ahead. If you want a couple of reminders about an event, you will have to set this up manually. Set the reminder that's furthest out—for example, one week. When that reminder appears in your email inbox, take a moment to go back and edit the event to add another reminder, such as one hour or one day ahead.

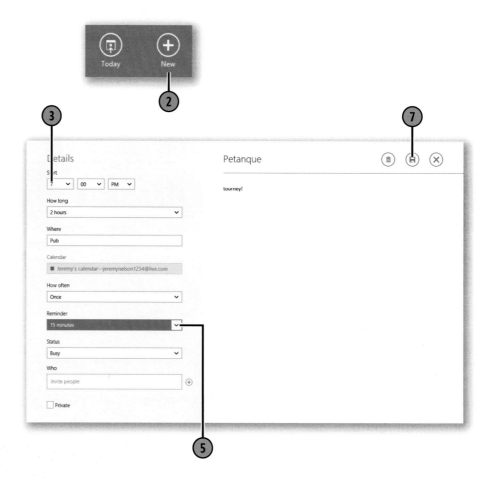

Inviting People to an Event

For many events, you will want to let other people know what's going on. When you set up an event such as a party or conference call, you can invite people to the event by entering their email addresses in the Details form. You can also enter a message that will go to all invitees.

Send an Invite

1 On the Start screen, click the Calendar app.

2 Click an existing event or right-click and then click New.

3 Click the Show More link.

4 Click in the Who field.

5 Enter and email address.

6 Click Send.

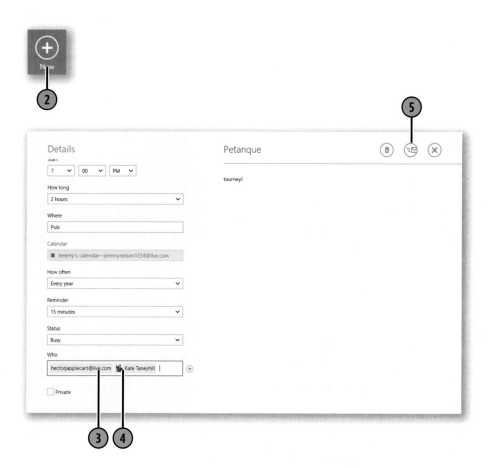

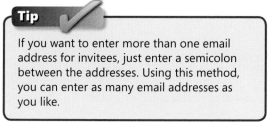

Tip

If you want to enter more than one email address for invitees, just enter a semicolon between the addresses. Using this method, you can enter as many email addresses as you like.

Editing an Existing Event

You can open an event's Details page and add or change information you've included there. For example, if the time of the event has changed or if you didn't know the location but now you do and want to add it, you can update these details. After you make the changes, simply save them and your event is up to date.

Edit Event Details

1. On the Start screen, click the Calendar app.

2. Click an event.

3. Click in a field, and modify the information as needed.

4. Click the Save this Event button.

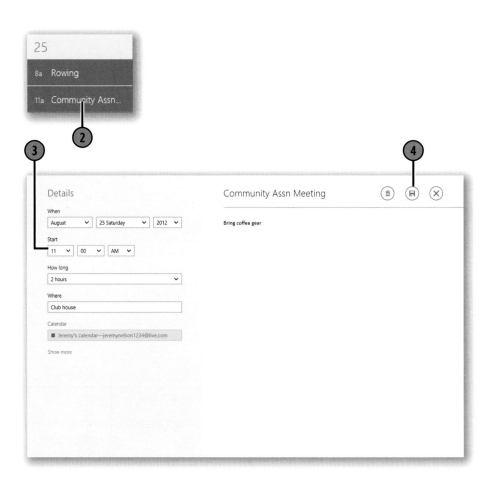

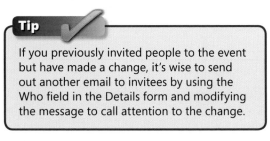

Tip

If you previously invited people to the event but have made a change, it's wise to send out another email to invitees by using the Who field in the Details form and modifying the message to call attention to the change.

Deleting an Event

Change is a constant in many of our lives. Luckily, the Calendar app helps you keep up with changes in your schedule. If an event such as a luncheon or business meeting gets canceled, it's best to delete it from your Calendar, especially if you've set it up to send you a reminder. You can delete an event from its Details page.

Delete an Event

1. On the Start screen, click the Calendar app.
2. Click an event.
3. Click the Delete Event button.
4. Click Delete to confirm.

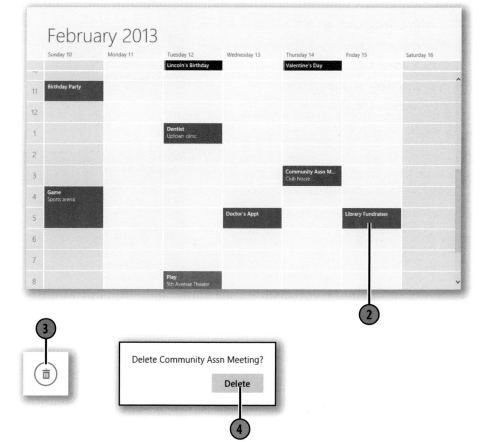

Tip ✓

When you click an event in your calendar, a pop-up offers you the choice of changing one event or all events. To delete all occurrences, click Change All and then use the preceding steps to delete them all.

February 2013

| Sunday 10 | Monday 11 | Tuesday 12 | Wednesday 13 | Thursday 14 | Friday 15 | Saturday 16 |

Lincoln's Birthday

Valentine's Day

Birthday Party

Dentist
Uptown clinic

Community Assn M...
Club house

Game
Sports arena

Doctor's Appt

Library Fundraiser

Play
5th Avenue Theater

Delete Community Assn Meeting?

Delete

Opening Weather in Different Views

The Weather app allows you to be prepared for what weather conditions will be in your location on any given day. You can display a few key points of data or more detailed information about the weather in a particular location, such as humidity and visibility. By default, Weather shows you only a week of weather forecasts, but you can view a few additional days beyond that.

Open and Explore the Weather App

1 On the Start screen, click the Weather app.

2 Click the More button. (If more information is already displayed, this button appears as a downward-facing arrow.)

3 Click the Less button. (If less information is already displayed, this button appears as an upward-facing arrow.)

4 Click the Forward arrow to scroll through a few more days of weather.

Tip

To change between temperature measurements in Celsius and Fahrenheit, right-click the Weather app screen and click the button in the lower-right corner, which will be labeled Change To Celsius if you're currently displaying Fahrenheit or Change To Fahrenheit if you're currently displaying Celsius.

Setting Up Location in Weather

Weather is a very useful app that helps you keep track of the weather where you are or the weather where you're headed. To get the correct forecast, you first have to indicate to the

Weather app the location for which you want a weather report. You can then get weather forecasts for just about any place in the world, in either Celsius or Fahrenheit.

Specify Your Location

1 On the Start screen, click the Weather app.

2 Right-click the screen.

3 Click Places.

4 Click the Add button.

5 Enter a location.

6 Click Add.

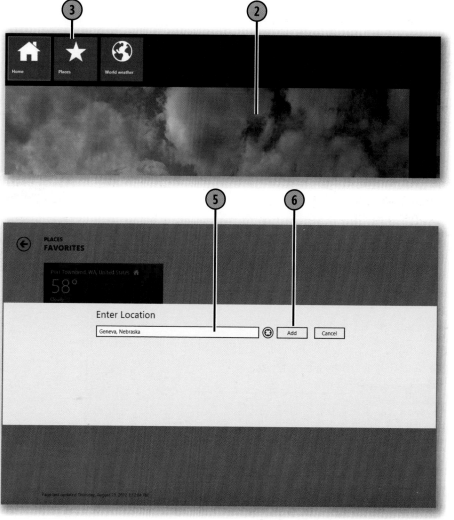

Tip

To set a location as your default location, with its weather displayed on the screen, right-click. Click the Set As Default button. Now when you right-click the screen in the Weather app and then click the Home button, your default location appears.

Reading Detailed Forecasts

When you display the Weather app, you see your default or last-displayed location and some weather details for the current date, such as temperature, wind, humidity, visibility, and the barometer reading. You can also choose to view detailed weather reports from one of two sources, which might include services, such as Foreca, Weather.com, Weather Underground, iMap Weather, or AccuWeather.

View Detailed Weather

① With the Weather app open, click the More button to display weather details.

② Click a weather service's name under today's weather to view that weather service.

③ Use the tools provided by your selected service to display hourly weather details or other information.

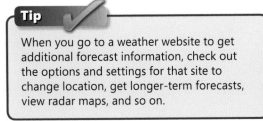

Tip

When you go to a weather website to get additional forecast information, check out the options and settings for that site to change location, get longer-term forecasts, view radar maps, and so on.

Viewing World Weather

The Weather app provides a shortcut for viewing weather in locations throughout the world. You can display a map of the world, with major cities in regions such as Europe, South America, Africa, and Australia called out. The world weather map doesn't offer every major city in the world, but it is a quick way

to see the weather around the world and jump to any major city that is displayed. (Remember, you can use the Places feature in the Weather app to view weather from any town or city in the world.)

Display World Weather Maps

1 With the Weather app open, right-click.

2 Click the World Weather button.

3 Click a city.

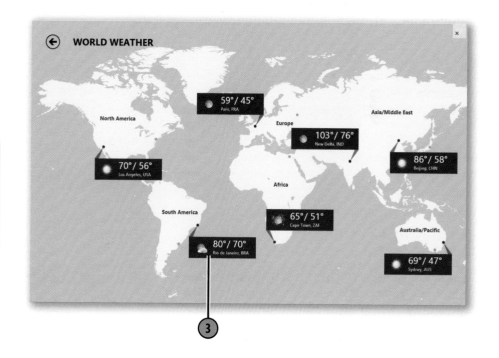

Tip

The display on the World Weather map alternates between two sets of major cities every few seconds. In Asia, for example, you can view Beijing, China or Tokyo, Japan. Just wait a few seconds to see the alternate cities appear.

16

Using the Maps App

Finding our way every day—to business meetings, luncheon appointments, concerts, or wherever—is one area of our lives where many of us have come to rely on a computing device. The Maps app comes pre-installed in Windows 8, and it offers some very easy-to-use and useful features.

Using the Maps app, you can pinpoint your computing device's current location (especially handy with laptops and tablets); get directions from point A to point B; get an aerial view of the world; and figure out how to avoid traffic on your morning or evening commute. The ability to zoom in and out for greater or lesser detail can be helpful in finding your way on a map. You can even get information about businesses and attractions, or jump quickly to online search results or related websites to find more details.

Opening and Navigating the Maps App

Imagine that you're headed out on a road trip with a paper map in hand. First you find your starting point, and then by unfolding and flipping the map around (trying not to whack the driver in the face), you figure out your route, if you're lucky. Today, electronic maps make life much easier. When you open the Maps app, you can zoom in and out to get more or less detail with a click, quickly find your current location, and then move the map around to find nearby locations with a simple click and drag action.

Open and Move Around Maps

1. Click the Maps tile.

2. Click to zoom in.

3. Click to zoom out.

4. To view adjacent areas, click and drag the map.

5. Right-click to display the toolbar.

6. To view the map of your current location, click My Location.

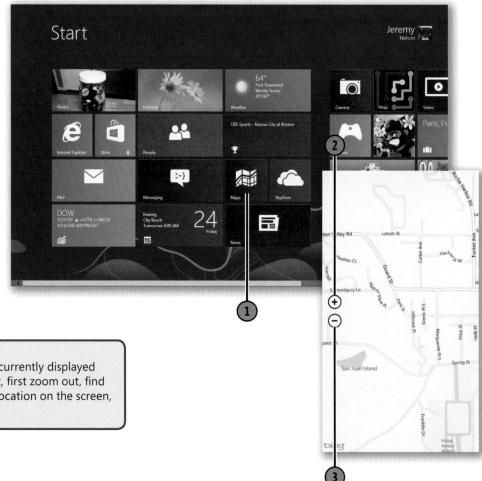

Tip

If you want to locate someplace near the currently displayed location but it's not visible at the moment, first zoom out, find the location, drag the map to center the location on the screen, and then zoom in again.

Choosing a Map Style

There are two views in the Maps app: Road View and Aerial View. The Road View is similar to a traditional road map with streets, bodies of water, and various landmarks represented as a simple two-dimensional illustration. The Aerial View is an actual photo of locations from the air, showing greenery, roads, and other topographical features. The view you display depends on what information you need.

Change Map Style

1. With the Maps app open, right-click to display the toolbar.

2. Click Map Style.

3. Click a view to apply it.

Tip

Aerial maps aren't shown in real time. Somebody took the picture perhaps a few months or years ago, so new construction or roads might not always appear accurately.

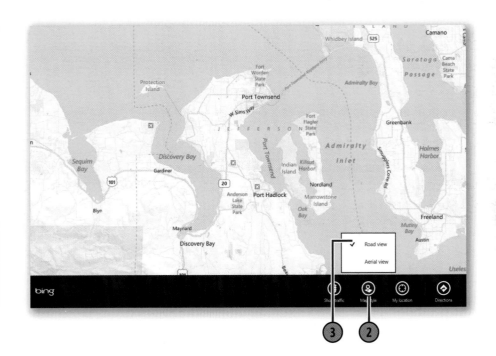

Searching for Locations

If you want to see a particular location displayed in the Maps app, you can simply enter an address using the Windows Integrated Search feature. The information you enter can be the name of a public landmark such as Hoover Dam, a city or town such as Denver, or a street address.

Search for a Location

① From the Start Screen, begin typing a search term such as "pizza".

② In the Search results, click Maps.

③ If there are multiple results, they appear at the top of the screen; click a result to go there.

④ Right-click to access Map tools to refine your search or get directions.

⑤ Right-click to display the Search field again.

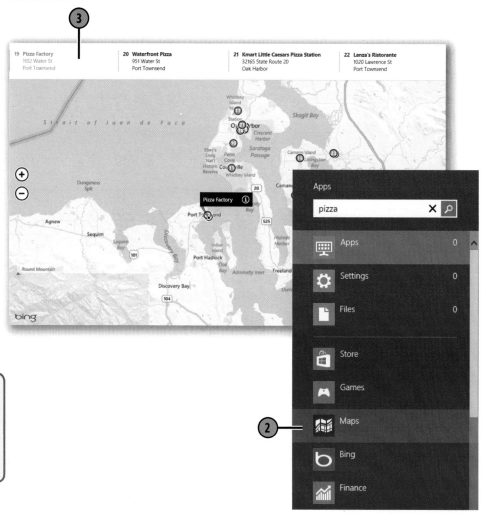

Try This!

You aren't limited to entering a city name or address in the Maps search field. Enter terms such as "Italian restaurant" or "Holiday Inn" to find nearby locations of a certain type or in a certain category.

Displaying Information About a Location

One of the wonderful features of the Maps app is the way it can tie into the Internet to provide details about a location, such as the hours and payment options for a restaurant or customer ratings for a hotel. You can even go to a website of a business by clicking a button in the Maps app.

Display Location Information

(1) With a location showing on a map, click the Information button.

(2) Click the Directions button to view directions to the location or click the Website button to go to a related website.

(3) Move your mouse to the upper-left corner of the screen, and click the Maps app in the Recent Sites area to return to the app.

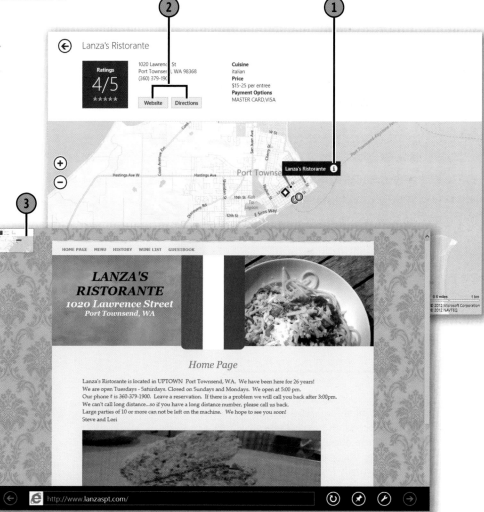

Tip

To allow apps like Maps to pinpoint your location, open the PC Settings screen, click Privacy, and then click the On/Off slider for Let Apps Use My Location.

Showing Traffic on Maps

If you live in a highly populated area, such as a major city, you can use the Traffic feature of the Maps app to display color codes for real-time traffic problems, as long as you have an Internet connection. Green roads are relatively clear, yellow roads have slowed traffic, and red roads have serious problems, with traffic slowing significantly.

Display Traffic

① On the Start screen, click the Maps app to open it.

② To display the toolbar, right-click.

③ If necessary, click Map Style.

Next, choose Road View.

④ Click the Show Traffic button.

⑤ To turn the feature off, click Show Traffic again.

Tip

Show Traffic isn't likely to work very well in smaller towns or rural areas where current traffic is seldom tracked, but in cities it can show you information about traffic jams, accidents, and other traffic problems on major arteries in virtually real time to help you find the best route.

Getting Directions

Looking at a map of a location can be helpful, but finding a route from one place to another is one of the major uses of a mapping program. By entering a start point and end point, the Maps app can calculate the route, tell you the total miles and time it will take to make the trip, and give you step-by-step directions.

Get Directions

1. With the Maps app open, right-click and then click Directions.

2. Click in the A field, and type a starting address or location.

3. Click in the B field, and type an ending address or location.

4. Click the Get Directions arrow.

5. To display the route on the map, click any segment in the directions.

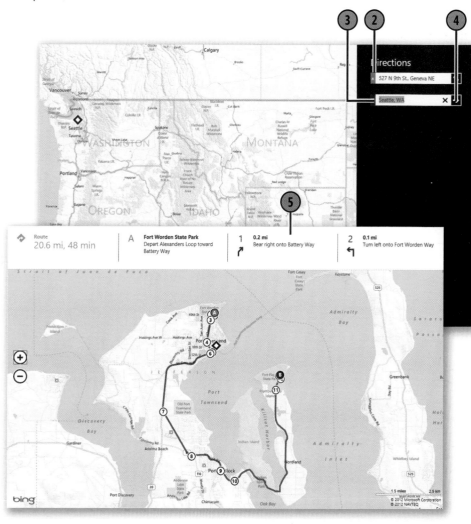

Tip ✓

To remove the route and clear the To and From fields, right-click to display the toolbar and then click the Clear Map button.

Tip ✓

To reverse the directions and switch the To and From locations, click the Direction arrows to the right of the first field. This is handy because on your return trip you might find that the directions differ slightly due to one-way roads or other routing anomalies.

Getting Visual

Computers aren't all about words and numbers. Today images, from photos to videos, provide a great way to share information and get creative.

Three pre-installed apps in Windows 8 help you take and manage photos and buy and play videos. If your computer or Windows 8–based computing device has a webcam capable of taking both still images and videos, you can record your own videos and play them back as well.

The Pictures, Video, and Camera apps are simple to use, but beyond the basics, they have a few bells and whistles also covered in this section, such as enabling you to run a slide show of photos or using a timer to take photos.

Displaying a Picture Library

Photos and other images on your computer are divided into libraries. You might have a library containing the contents of the Pictures folder on your computer, another of Facebook photos, and another containing any images that you've stored at a popular online photo sharing site (Flickr, for example).

Open a Picture Library

1. On the Start screen, click the Photos tile.
2. To move through your libraries, click the arrow to the right of the scroll bar.
3. Click a library to open it.
4. To scroll through the photos in the library, click the arrow in the lower-right corner of the screen.
5. Click the arrow in the bottom-left corner of the screen to scroll back through the library.
6. To enlarge a photo to full screen, click it.

> **Tip** ✓
>
> When you've enlarged a photo to full screen, arrows appear in the middle of the right and left screens; use these to move back to the previous image or forward to the next image in the library.

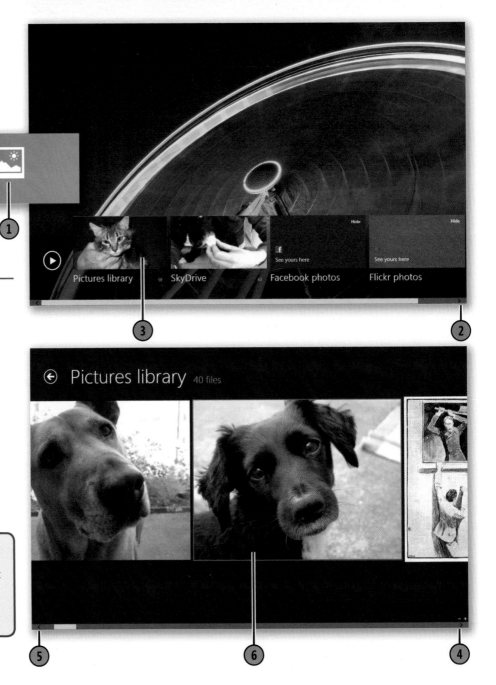

Using a Photo as an App Tile or Lock Screen

You might want to replace an existing solid-colored tile with a tile containing a photo background to spice up the look of the Start screen. You might also want to use an image in Photos as the background for the Lock screen that displays when your computer is sleeping. You can use the Photos app to apply these settings.

Set a Photo as an App Tile or Lock Screen

1. On the Start screen, click the Photos app tile.

2. Locate the photo you want (see previous task), and double-click it.

3. Right-click.

4. Click Set As.

5. Click App Tile or Lock Screen.

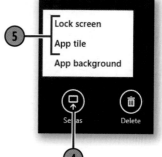

Searching for a Photo

The Search feature of Windows 8 allows you to search for apps, settings, and files. If you have a picture file stored on your hard disk or on an external storage device, such as on a USB flash drive, you can use the Search feature to search by the file name or associated keywords.

Search for Photos

① On the Start screen, type the title of a photo file.

② In the Search results, click Files.

③ Click Pictures.

④ Click the picture you want the Photos app to display when you open the app.

⑤ To move to the previous or next picture, click the right or left arrow.

⑥ To return to the Photos main screen, press Escape.

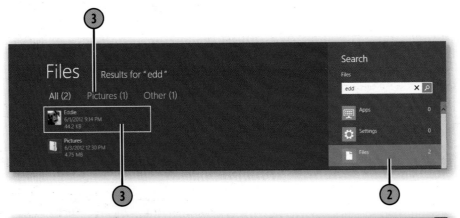

Tip

When you display the contents of your Pictures Library, which is the Pictures folder on your hard disk, you can right-click and click the Browse By Date button to display images from most recent to least recent.

Running a Slide Show

The Photos slide show feature is just what it sounds like: Windows displays one image after another automatically. You can select a set of images to play in a slide show, which can be useful for giving sales presentations or sharing personal images with friends.

Run a Slide Show

① On the Start screen, click the Photos tile.

② Click to open a library.

③ Right-click.

④ Click Slide Show.

⑤ To stop the slide show, click anywhere on the screen.

Tip

A slide show will run through all the photos in a library and then cycle through them again. There is no way to pause the slide show; you can only start and stop it.

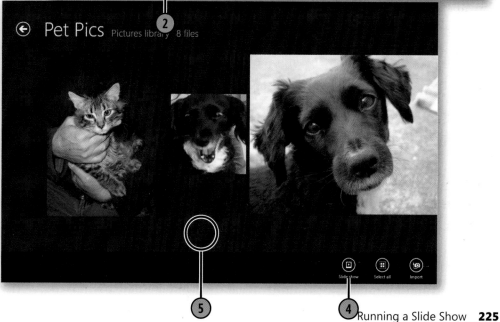

Buying or Renting a Video

The Video app gives you access to videos in the Windows Store. You can either rent or buy videos and play them back in the Video app. You have to register a credit card and purchase Microsoft points to buy or rent videos.

Buy or Rent Videos

1. On the Start screen, click the Video tile.

2. Click the Movies Store or TV Store category.

3. To move through the selections, click the right arrow to the right of the scroll bar.

4. Click an item.

5. Click the Explore button.

   (Click Explore Series for TV, and click Explore Movie for movies; you might also have to click a View Seasons link to view TV seasons and then click on a specific episode.).

6. Click the Buy button or the Rent button.

7. If you need to purchase Microsoft Points, click the Buy Points button and follow the instructions.

8. Click the Confirm button.

Tip

You can click the links at the top of a marketplace, such as Top, Genres, or Networks at the top of the TV Marketplace page, to view different categories that can help you find the selection you want.

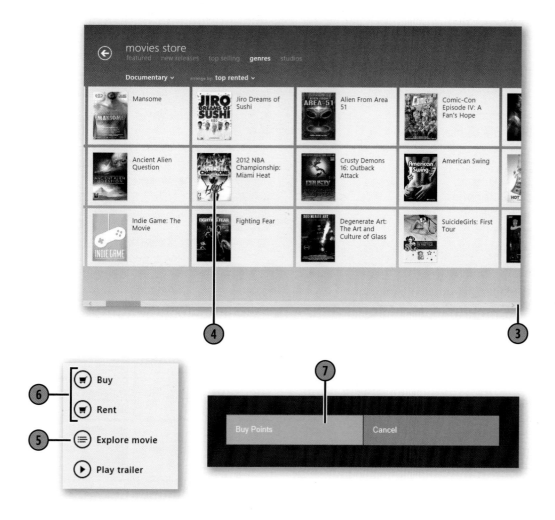

Finding a Video

After you've taken your own videos or purchased videos, you'll accumulate a video collection. Before you can play a video, you have to find the one you want by browsing your collection in the Video app.

Browse Your Videos

① On the Start screen, click the Video tile.

② Click My Videos.

③ To view items in specific categories, click the Movies Store, Television Store, or Other link to view items in these categories.

④ Click the Date Added link.

⑤ To view items alphabetically, click A to Z.

Tip

You can also simply begin to type the title of a video on the Start screen and use the Files category to search for the file if you've downloaded it to your computer.

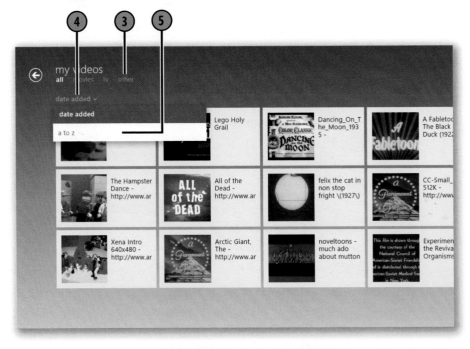

Playing a Video

The Video app offers several controls for playing your videos that will seem familiar to anybody who has used a movie player before. You can play, pause, stop, fast forward, or rewind your video selection by using these simple tools.

Play a Video

1. When you find the item you want to play by using the steps in the previous task, click it.

2. Click the Play button.

3. Click the Pause button to pause.

4. Click and drag the progress bar to move to another location in the video.

5. Right-click the screen to display playback tools.

6. Click the Previous button to go back.

7. Click the Next button to go forward.

8. Click the Repeat button to watch the video again.

Tip ✓

Click the icon at the bottom-right of the screen when on-screen playback tools are visible, to reduce the size of the playback window and to view the video description. Click the video again, and click the same tool to return to a full screen display.

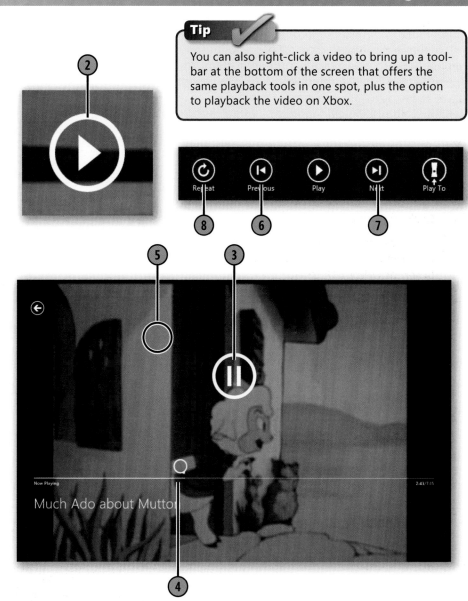

Tip ✓

You can also right-click a video to bring up a toolbar at the bottom of the screen that offers the same playback tools in one spot, plus the option to playback the video on Xbox.

Repeat   Previous   Play   Next   Play To

Now Playing

2:43/7:15

Much Ado about Mutton

Using the Camera

Assuming your computing device has a built-in webcam, you can use that camera to take photos and videos. You can use settings in the Camera app of Windows 8 to choose which mode to use, camera or video, and to select from a small set of resolution options.

Change Camera and Camera Mode

Sometimes you want to take still photos, and at other times you want to record a video, and if you have a device that has both front-facing and back-facing cameras, you need to choose which camera mode to use. Changing between the photo and video modes is a simple matter of a mouse click (or, if you're lucky enough to have a touchscreen, a tap on the screen).

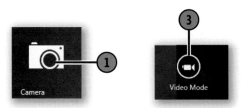

1. On the Start screen, click the Camera tile.

2. To change between front-facing and back-facing cameras if your computing device has both, click the Change Camera button.

3. To switch between video (white background) and still camera (black background), click the Video Mode button.

Set Camera Resolution

Resolution affects the clarity of images that you capture—the higher the resolution, the better the appearance of the images. The Camera app in Windows 8 allows a small but useful choice of resolutions.

1 On the Start screen, click the Camera tile.

2 Click the Camera Options button.

3 On the Resolution field, click the arrow.

4 Click a resolution.

5 To close the Camera Options dialog box, click outside it.

Tip

If you click More Options in the Camera Options dialog box, you can use sliders to control the brightness and contrast in your images, the flicker rate in your videos, and the focus and exposure settings for your camera(s).

Capturing Images

The process of actually taking a photo or recording a video is very simple. You open the Camera app, choose which mode you want to shoot in, and then click the screen to take the photo or start the video recording. After you take photos or videos by using the Camera app, you will find them in the Webcam folder of the Photos app.

Take a Photo

1. On the Start screen, click the Camera tile.
2. If you need to change to still photos, click the Video mode button.
3. Click the screen to take this photo.
4. To view the photo you just took, at the left edge of the screen, click the Back arrow.

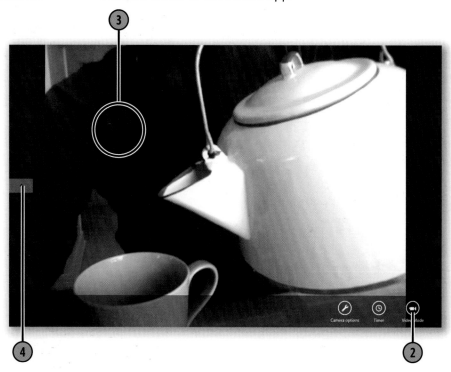

Tip

If you prefer a countdown before your camera begins capturing photos or videos, click the Timer button on the Camera app toolbar. This turns a timer on or off. With the timer on, a three second countdown is displayed on your screen when you click to activate either camera.

Record a Video

1. On the Start screen, click the Camera tile.

2. If you need to change to video mode, click the Video mode button.

3. Click the screen.

4. When you're finished recording, click the screen again.

5. To display the video you just recorded, at the left edge of the screen, click the arrow.

6. To play the video, click the playback arrow.

Tip

When you play back a video, a Trim button and Delete button appear at the bottom of the screen. Use the first to slide the indicators on the progress bar to the left or right to shorten the video, and use the second to delete the video.

Playing Music

In Windows 8, you have two choices for playing and organizing your music: the new Music app and the Windows Media Player, which you might have used in previous versions of Windows. Both allow you to play music, but beyond that, they have different strengths.

The Music app is a great way to look for and buy new music, as well as sort music into different categories to help you find selections. The app's opening screen offers Spotlight (featured selections you can explore), Collection (music you own), and Music Marketplace (the place to shop for music). You can use the Music app to buy music from Zune Marketplace, Microsoft's music store, using points you purchase.

The Windows Media Player, on the other hand, makes organizing music and creating playlists easy, and for some, it offers the added benefit of providing a familiar interface and familiar tools.

Whichever app you use, you'll be able to enjoy all your favorite music and find new selections to fill out your music library.

Navigating the Music App

The Music app is probably completely new to you; it has a different look and feel from other music players you've used. It's more than a player—it's a music store as well. In this task, you begin to find your way around the Music app by using the Windows 8 interface.

Navigate the Music App

1. On the Start screen, click the Music app.

2. To move from My Music to other suggested selections of music you can shop for, click and drag the scroll bar to the right.

3. Click a selection in My Music, and it opens and begins playing.

4. To display tools, right-click the screen.

5. To stop the current selection from playing, click the Pause button.

6. To return to the Start screen, press the Windows logo key.

Try This!

You can also get to the music app by searching for music. On the Start screen, begin typing the name of a song, artist, or album. In the Search screen that appears, finish entering your search term and click the Music category. The Music app opens and displays information about the music, artist, or album. You can now preview or buy the selection. (See the next task.)

Finding Music to Buy

You can use the Windows 8 Search feature to find music, but you can also use tools in the Music app itself to find music that interests you in the Marketplace. A variety of sorting criteria helps you to locate the type of music you like or a particular artist.

Locate Music

1. On the Start screen, click the Music app.
2. Click a category name such as Xbox Music Store or Most Popular.
3. On the All Genres list, click a genre.
4. When you find a selection you like, click and drag the scroll bar up or down.
5. Click the selection.
6. Click outside the selection to close it.

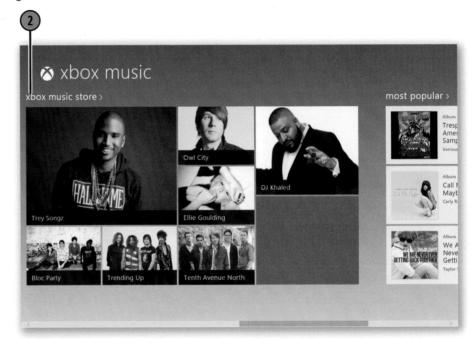

Tip

If you know the name of the song or album you want to buy, using the Windows 8 Search feature is probably a quicker way to find the selection you seek.

Previewing Music

The Music app lets you get a preview of music you might be interested in. This feature lets you listen to snippets of selections in an album so that you can decide whether you like it enough to buy. When you preview an album, a short portion of a song plays and then the Music app moves on to the next track, and so on, through the selected album.

Preview a Selection

① When you've found a selection you want to preview, click it.

② Click Preview.

③ To stop the preview, click Pause.

④ Click outside the preview window to return to the marketplace.

Tip

There is no volume setting in the Music app playback tools. To adjust volume, press Windows logo key+I, click the Volume control in the Settings panel, and then move the slider up or down.

Buying Points

When you buy music using the Music app, you are buying from the Zune online store. This store uses points for your purchases. You buy a certain number of points, and then when you shop, you redeem those points to make your purchases. So the first step in acquiring any music in the Marketplace is to buy some points.

Buy Points

1. Locate an item in Marketplace, and click it.

2. Click Buy Album.

3. Click Buy Points.

4. Click the option showing the number of points you want to purchase.

5. Click Next.

6. Click Add A New Credit Card if you haven't added one already.

7. Enter the card information.

8. Click Save.

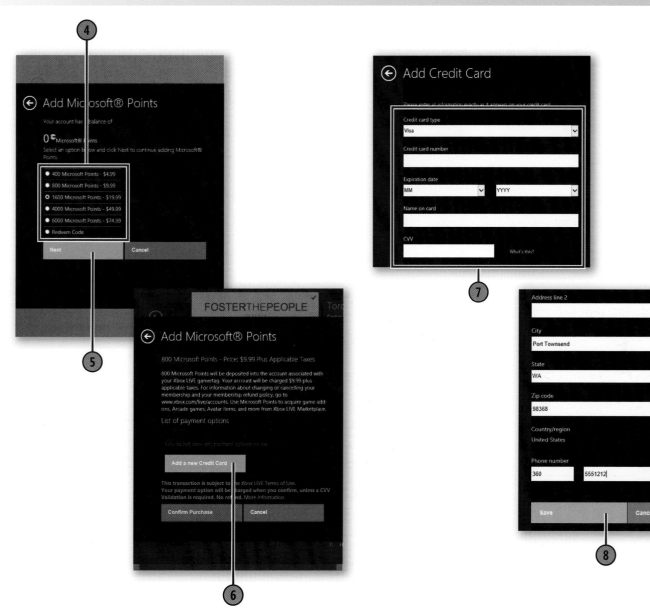

Buying Music

After you've purchased some points, you can begin to redeem those points to buy music. Buying is as simple as making your selection, clicking to buy it, and if required, entering the verification code from your credit card. The purchased music is then available in your Collection in the Music app.

Buy a Selection

1. In the Xbox Music Store, click a selection.

2. Click Buy Album.

3. Click Confirm.

4. Enter your credit card verification value if requested.

For information about shopping at the Windows Store for apps, see Section 14, "Buying Apps at the Windows Store."

Listening to Music

The whole point of finding and buying music is to listen to it. The pleasing interface and simple playback tools in the Music app make listening to your music a very pleasant experience.

Play Music

(1) With the Music app open, click an item in My Music.

(2) To display playback controls, right-click the screen.

(3) To go to the next track, click Next.

(4) To go to the previous track, click Previous.

(5) To repeat a track before it ends, click Repeat.

(6) To move among tracks in a random way, click Shuffle.

(7) To pause the music, click Pause.

Tip

Note that if you used Windows Media Center in the past to play content in Windows 8, this feature has become a desktop app that you need to download to use.

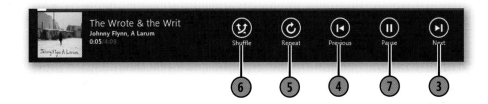

Playing Music with Windows Media Player

Windows Media Player offers another way to organize and play music on your computer or from a DVD, as well as offering a way to play videos and view photos. One big plus with Win-dows Media Player is that it provides an easy way to create and play music from playlists, your own customized lists of music.

Play Music

① On the Start screen, type **Windows Media Player**.

② In the search results, click Windows Media Player.

③ To display your music, click Music.

④ To play a selection, double-click it.

⑤ To go to the next selection, click the Next button.

⑥ To go to the previous selection, click the Previous button.

⑦ To play songs in a random way, click the Shuffle button.

⑧ To repeat a selection while it's play-ing, click the Turn Repeat On button.

⑨ To adjust the volume control, click and drag it.

Tip

While playing music, you can click the Now Playing button in the lower-right corner to display a window with controls for the currently playing selection. Click the Switch To Library button in the upper-right corner to go back to the Media Player main screen. You might have to move your mouse over the window to make the Switch To Library and other tool buttons appear.

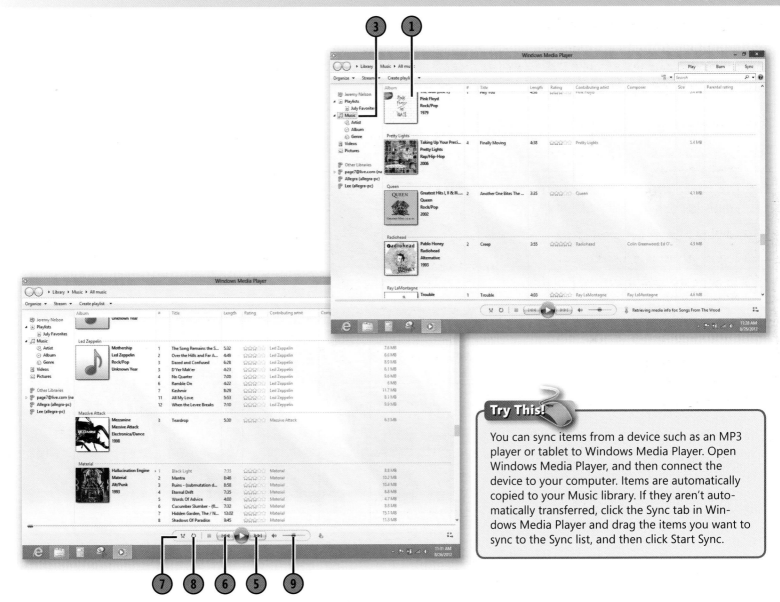

You can sync items from a device such as an MP3 player or tablet to Windows Media Player. Open Windows Media Player, and then connect the device to your computer. Items are automatically copied to your Music library. If they aren't automatically transferred, click the Sync tab in Windows Media Player and drag the items you want to sync to the Sync list, and then click Start Sync.

Organizing Music

In Windows Media Player, you can sort items in your music library and playlists by various criteria such as Title, Artist, Composer, or Length. You can also view music selections by categories such as Artist, Album, and Genre.

Sort Music

1. With Windows Media Player and the Music library open, Click Organize.

2. Click Sort By.

3. Click a criterion to sort by.

4. To display music by category, in the Music library, click the Artist, Album, or Genre options.

Tip

If you have inserted an audio DVD into your computer and want to copy the files from it to Windows Media Player, click the album in the left pane of the player, and click the Burn tab on the right pane. Click Rip, and all songs are copied to your music library.

Creating Playlists

Most of us enjoy various artists and even genres of music, and our favorite songs or pieces might come from a variety of sources. Playlists let you pick and choose pieces of music from various sources to make your own mix. One might be romantic, another great for dancing, and still another might be the list of music you'd choose to be shipwrecked with on a desert island. Playlists are all about customizing your music experience, and they're easy to create.

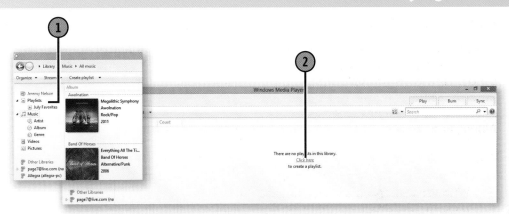

Create a Playlist

① With Windows Media Player open, click Playlists.

② To create a playlist, click the Click Here link.

③ Enter a name for the playlist.

④ To save the name, click outside the playlist name field.

⑤ To add a selection to the new playlist, right-click the desired selection.

⑥ Click Add to.

⑦ Click the playlist name to which to add the selection.

⑧ To add additional selections to the playlist, repeat steps 5 through 7.

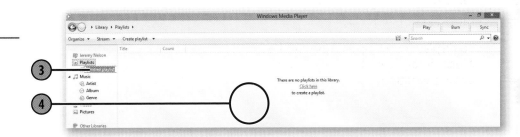

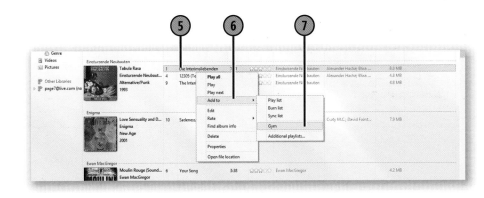

Playing Playlists

After you've created a few playlists, it's time to listen to your selections. The playback controls for playlists are the same as those covered earlier in the "Playing Music with Windows Media Player" task.

Play Back Your Playlists

1. With Windows Media Player open, click Playlists.

2. To open a playlist, double-click it.

3. To play a title in the playlist, double-click it.

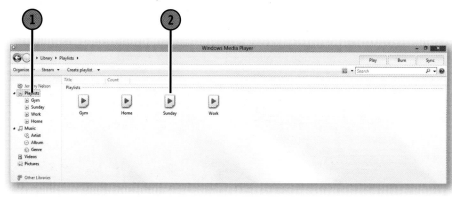

Try This!

You can edit a playlist at any time by using several options. Click the playlist and on the Play tab on the right side of the window, click and drag a song up or down to reorder the items in the playlist. Click the Clear List button to clear all items in the list. Click the List Options button, and shuffle or sort the list by using the commands in the menu that appears. You can also right-click an item on the list and choose Remove From List to remove it.

19

Working with Devices and Networks

Your Windows operating system not only lets you play with apps galore, it helps your computer interface with hardware such as printers and scanners. You might be called on to help Windows connect by following a simple procedure to add a new device or by checking to see whether your device driver is current.

You can use Bluetooth technology to connect to devices at a short range, such as a wireless keyboard that sits on your desk next to your computer.

In addition to connecting to other devices, you might want to connect your computer to other computers. This can be done by setting up a wireless network. Devices that connect to your network can share a printer, Internet connection, and more.

Adding a Device

If you have a printer that you want to use with your computer, you first need to establish a connection between the two. This involves following the Add A Device procedure, which, in most cases, automatically identifies any attached devices. As you work your way through the Add A Device process, you might need to search for or download a driver for the printer and make a choice about how you want to share the printer on a network.

Add a Device

① Press Windows logo key+I.

② Click Change PC Settings and then click Devices.

③ Click Add a Device.

④ In the list that appears, click a printer.

⑤ Click Next.

⑥ Enter a different printer name if you prefer.

⑦ Click Next.

⑧ Select the printer sharing setting you prefer, and enter any required information.

⑨ Click Next.

⑩ Click Print a Test Page.

⑪ Click Finish.

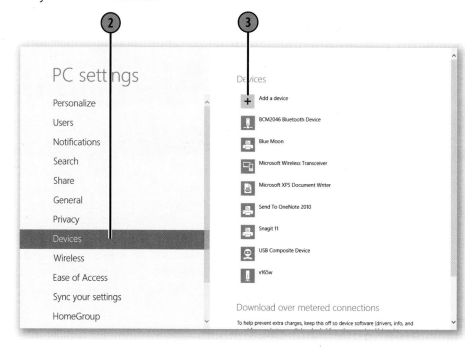

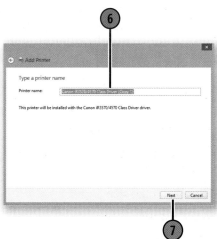

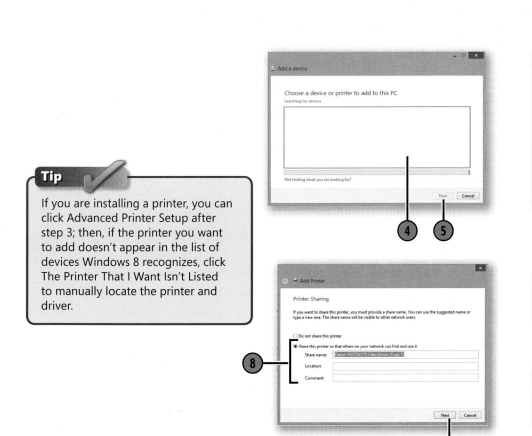

Tip

If you are installing a printer, you can click Advanced Printer Setup after step 3; then, if the printer you want to add doesn't appear in the list of devices Windows 8 recognizes, click The Printer That I Want Isn't Listed to manually locate the printer and driver.

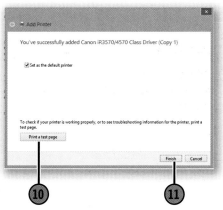

Connecting to Bluetooth Devices

Bluetooth is a technology that allows you to connect to Bluetooth-enabled devices that are within a short range of your computer. For example, you might connect to a Bluetooth mouse or keyboard placed a few feet or less from your computer. This involves making sure that both devices have Bluetooth on and that the devices are discoverable, which you can manage by applying a simple setting.

Make Your Computer Discoverable

1. On a computer with Bluetooth capability, type **Control Panel** on the Start screen.

2. In the Search results, click Control Panel.

3. In the Search box, type **Bluetooth**.

4. Click Change Bluetooth Settings.

5. Click Allow Bluetooth Devices To Find This Computer.

6. Click OK.

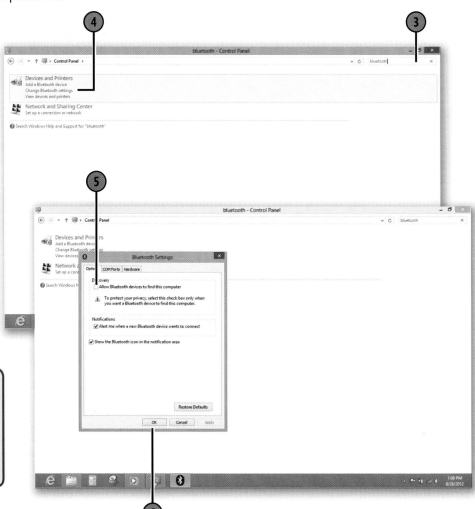

Tip

When you don't need to connect to a Bluetooth device, it's a good idea to turn Bluetooth off, especially if you're traveling around with you laptop. Otherwise, there's a risk that someone might use a device like a tablet or phone to tap into your computer's contents or settings.

Connect to Bluetooth Devices

① On the start screen, type **Control Panel** and tap Apps.

② In the Search results, click Control Panel.

③ In the Search box, type Bluetooth.

④ Click Add a Bluetooth Device.

⑤ Click a device.

⑥ Click Next.

⑦ Verify that the displayed passcode on your computer and Bluetooth device match, and click Yes.

⑧ Click Close.

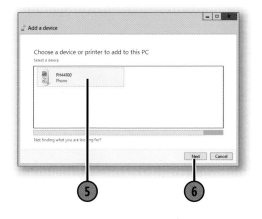

Setting Up a Homegroup

Home networks use a homegroup to include computers in the network. When you belong to a homegroup, you can share files and printers among those in the group. Others can't change files that you share unless you give them permission to do so. You can create a new homegroup, or you can join a homegroup that's been set up on another computer in your network.

Join a Homegroup

1. Press Windows logo key+I.
2. Click Change PC Settings.
3. Click HomeGroup.
4. If a homegroup is already set up, your computer might find it; if not, enter a homegroup password.
5. Click Join.

Tip

The administrator of your network can view the password and share it with you by going to the Control Panel, clicking Network And Internet, HomeGroup, and then clicking View Or Print The HomeGroup Password.

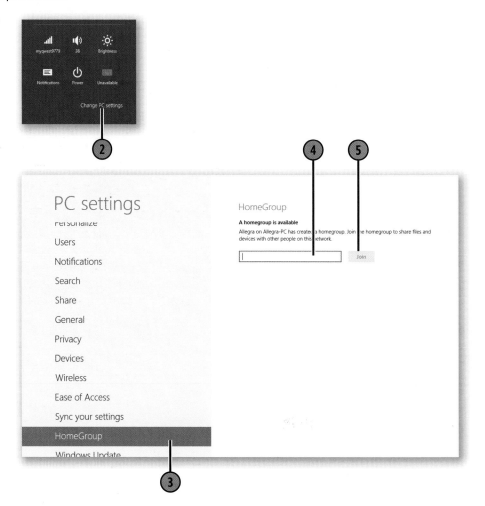

myqwest9779   3B   Brightness

Notifications   Power   Unavailable

Change PC settings

PC settings

Personalize
Users
Notifications
Search
Share
General
Privacy
Devices
Wireless
Ease of Access
Sync your settings
HomeGroup
Windows Update

HomeGroup

A homegroup is available
Allegra on Allegra-PC has created a homegroup. Join the homegroup to share files and devices with other people on this network.

Join

Connecting to a Network

It's especially handy to be able to log in to different networks if you move around with a laptop or tablet device. You can take advantage of the many free hot spots in cafés and other public places to go online when you know how to connect to them.

Connect to an Available Network

1 Click Windows logo key+I.

2 Click the network button.

3 Click a network name.

4 Click Connect.

Tip

To have your computer connect to this network whenever it's in range, select the Connect Automatically check box before clicking Connect in step 4.

Choosing What to Share on a Network

You can share various items with other computers on your network, such as printers or libraries of documents. You can also share media content on your computer with another media device such as a tablet.

Set Up Sharing

1. Press Windows logo key+I.

2. Click Change PC Settings.

3. Click HomeGroup.

4. Assuming you are a member of a homegroup, you will see various settings. Click the On/Off button for any of the Libraries or Devices listed.

5. To share content with media devices, click the On/Off button.

Tip

Don't worry about others on your network changing your content. Sharing content allows others only to view your documents, not modify them.

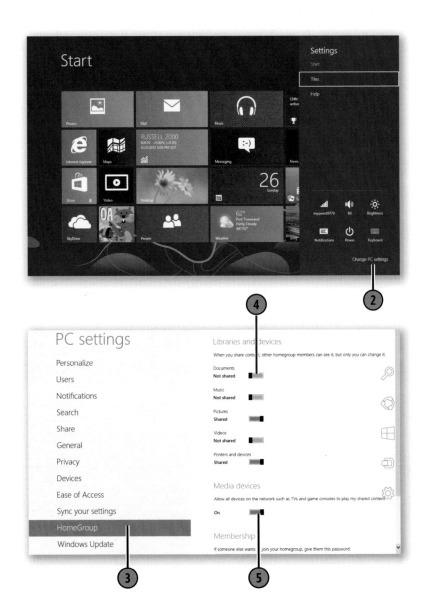

Tethering Your Computer to Your Cell Phone

If you have a smartphone with the ability to provide a personal hot spot, you can use your phone's 3G connection to get your computer online. Having this ability on your phone typically involves an additional monthly fee, and your computer must have Wi-Fi capability.

Connect to the Internet Using Your Cell Phone

1. Turn on Hotspot from your phone.
2. Press Windows logo key+I.
3. Click the network button.
4. Click your phone's Wi-Fi connection.
5. Click Connect.
6. Enter the Security Key.
7. Click Next.
8. Click an option to turn sharing on or off.

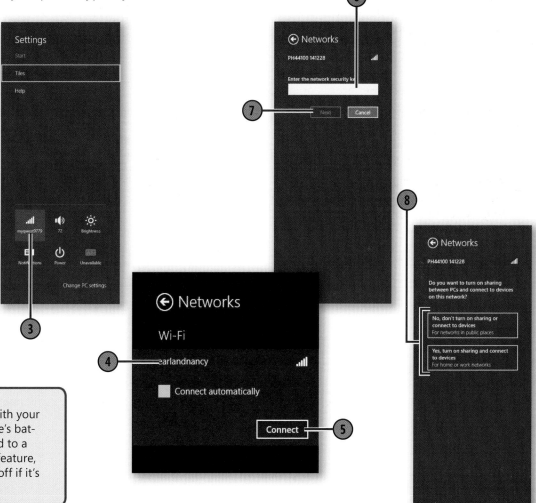

Tip

Using your smartphone to go online with your computer can quickly drain your phone's battery. Try to have your phone connected to a power source when using its hot spot feature, and turn the phone's hot spot feature off if it's not in use.

Setting Up a Wireless Network

Many people find it convenient to set up a home network. With such a network in place, you can allow devices that join the network to share a printer connection, Internet access, documents in shared folders, and more.

Set Up a Wireless Network

1. Connect a router or other access point hardware to your computer, and type **Control Panel** on the Start screen.

2. In the Search results, click Control Panel.

3. Click Network And Internet.

4. Click Network And Sharing Center.

5. Click Set Up A New Connection Or Network.

6. Click Set Up A New Network.

7. Click Next.

8. Click the router or access point that you want to set up.

9. Click Next.

10. Enter your PIN number located on the router label.

11. Click Next.

12. Enter a name for the network.

13. Click Next.

14. When the setup completes, click Close.

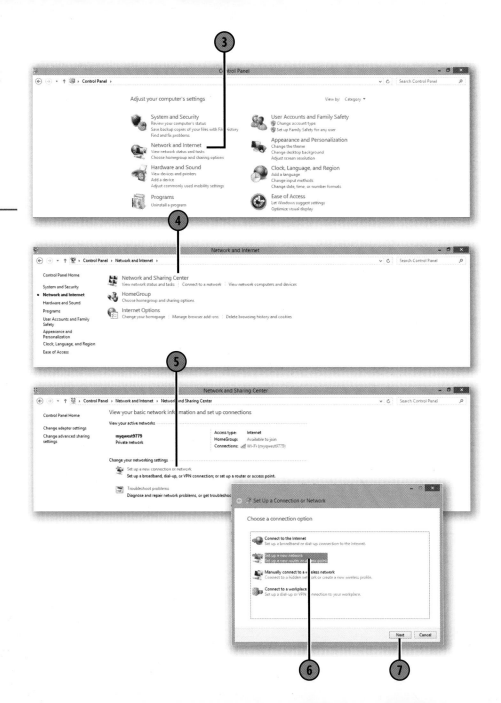

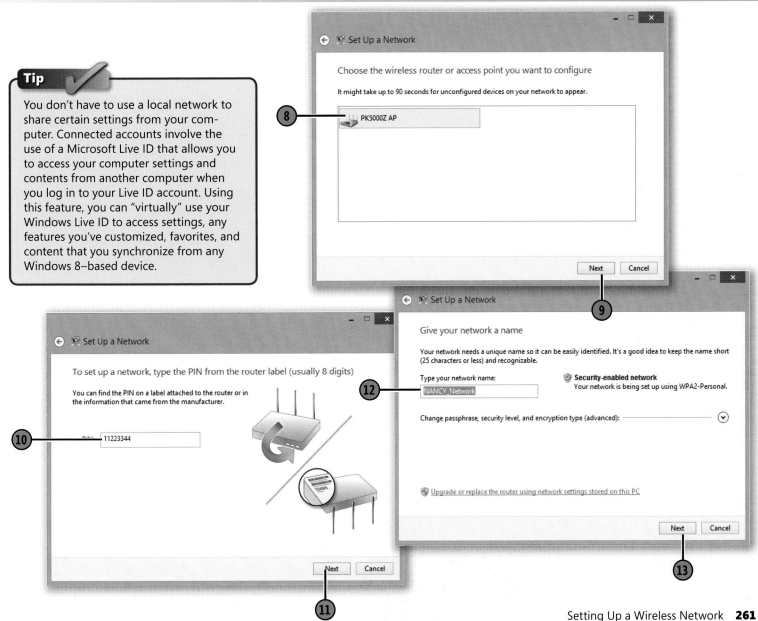

Tip

You don't have to use a local network to share certain settings from your computer. Connected accounts involve the use of a Microsoft Live ID that allows you to access your computer settings and contents from another computer when you log in to your Live ID account. Using this feature, you can "virtually" use your Windows Live ID to access settings, any features you've customized, favorites, and content that you synchronize from any Windows 8–based device.

Set Up a Network

Choose the wireless router or access point you want to configure

It might take up to 90 seconds for unconfigured devices on your network to appear.

PK5000Z AP

Next   Cancel

Set Up a Network

To set up a network, type the PIN from the router label (usually 8 digits)

You can find the PIN on a label attached to the router or in the information that came from the manufacturer.

PIN: 11223344

Next   Cancel

Set Up a Network

Give your network a name

Your network needs a unique name so it can be easily identified. It's a good idea to keep the name short (25 characters or less) and recognizable.

Type your network name:

NANCY_Network

Security-enabled network
Your network is being set up using WPA2-Personal.

Change passphrase, security level, and encryption type (advanced):

Upgrade or replace the router using network settings stored on this PC

Next   Cancel

Maintaining and Troubleshooting Your Computer

Windows 8 has several built-in features with which you can keep your computer system running at its best or to help you restore your computer if it experiences a problem. You can use these tools to get Windows operating system updates that can fix security vulnerabilities, clear out unused bits of data from your hard disk to improve performance, back up your data, and restart your computer in the case of a computer crash.

If you aren't that technically savvy and feel you need help troubleshooting your computer, try using the Remote Assistance feature in Windows 8. With this feature, you can invite someone using another computer to access your computer and help you solve your problem.

In this section, you discover how to use various tools in PC Settings and the Control Panel to keep your computer performing optimally.

Setting Up Windows Updates

Periodically, Microsoft sends out updates to its operating system to make improvements or fix problems that have surfaced. You can set Windows 8 to download and install these updates automatically. You can also choose to just have the most urgent updates downloaded to your computer.

Update Windows Automatically

1. On the Start screen, begin to type **Control Panel**.

2. Click the Control Panel app in the results.

3. Click System And Security.

4. Click Turn Automatic Updating On Or Off.

5. Click the drop-down arrow in the Important Updates field and choose Install Updates Automatically, which is Microsoft's recommended setting.

6. If you prefer, select the Recommended Updates check box to have less-important updates installed.

7. Click OK.

Tip

If you'd rather have more control over downloaded updates, you can choose either the Download Updates But Let Me Choose Whether To Install Them, or the Check For Updates But Let Me Choose Whether To Download And Install Them option. These options enable you to pick and choose among the updates, downloading only those you need.

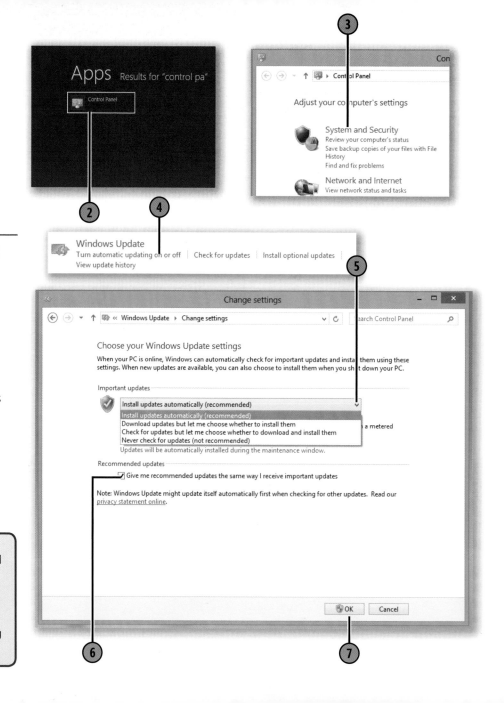

Checking for Updates

If you don't choose to download updates automatically or you don't want to wait for the next automatic update, you can initiate an update manually. Windows 8 then checks for any updates that are available at that time. In some cases, Windows requires that you restart your computer after downloading updates.

Update Windows Manually

① Press Windows logo key+I.

② Click Change PC Settings.

③ Click Windows Update.

④ Click Check For Updates Now.

⑤ Click Install.

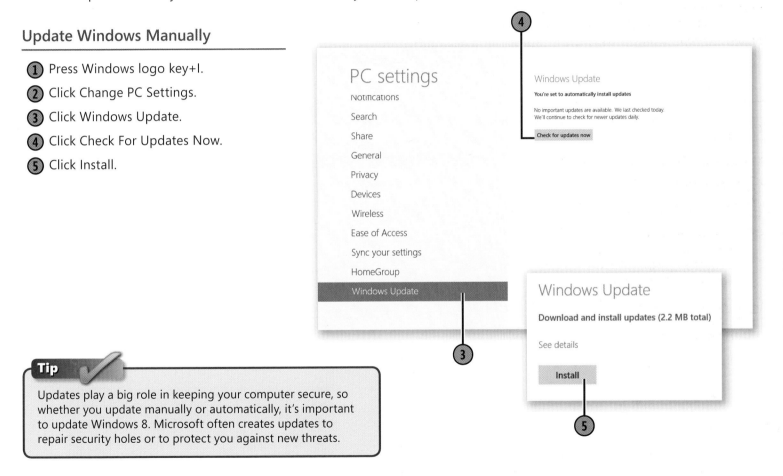

Tip

Updates play a big role in keeping your computer secure, so whether you update manually or automatically, it's important to update Windows 8. Microsoft often creates updates to repair security holes or to protect you against new threats.

Resetting Windows 8

Resetting Windows 8 to factory settings is a last-ditch effort to get a damaged system back up to speed. You might also want to reset a computer before selling it to somebody else so that your files and apps are unavailable to them. When you reset Windows 8, any files you created or any apps you downloaded will be gone. All Windows 8 settings will be returned to the default settings.

Reset Windows 8

1. Press Windows logo key+I.

2. Click Change PC Settings.

3. Click General.

4. Scroll down in the right pane.

5. Under Remove Everything And Reinstall Windows, click the Get Started button.

6. On the next screen, click Next.

7. Click either Only The Drive Where Windows Is Installed or All Drives.

8. Click Thoroughly or Quickly, depending on how important it is that all files be recoverable.

9. Click Reset.

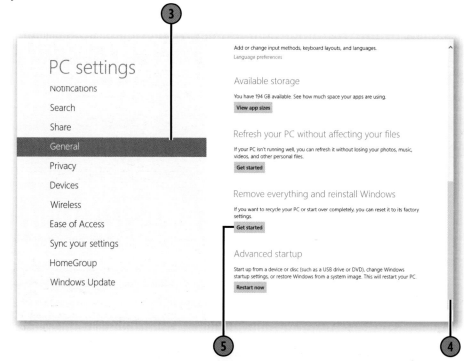

Tip

If you decide at any point during the reset procedure that you don't want to do a reset (and lose all your files and settings), just click the Cancel button.

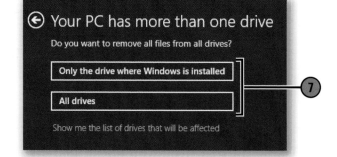

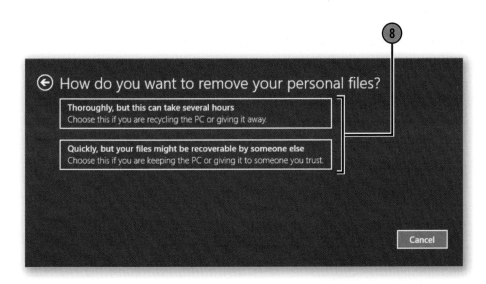

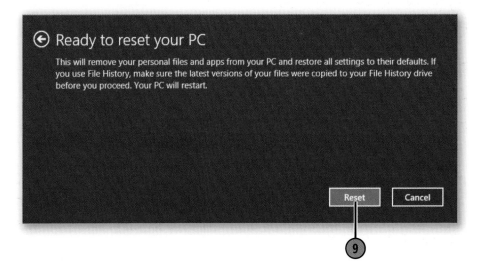

Using Advanced Startup

If Windows is somehow corrupted or experiencing a problem, one option is to restart it but have the system boot up (retrieve the system settings) from a source other than your computer. You can choose to use a USB stick or DVD that contains either the Windows operating system or a system image that you've saved so that you can get the system working and troubleshoot any problems.

Booting Your Computer from a Disc

① Place a USB stick or DVD that contains the Windows software or a system image in your computer.

② Press Windows logo key+I.

③ Click Change PC Settings.

④ Click General.

⑤ Scroll down the right pane.

⑥ Under Advanced Startup, click Restart Now.

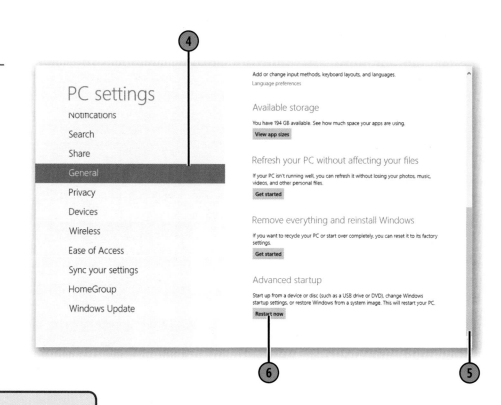

Tip

If you forget to insert media into your computer to boot up from, don't worry. Windows will bring up a screen giving you the option to exit and load Windows 8 the traditional way.

Refreshing Your PC

If you want to try to clean up any buggy behavior on the part of Windows 8 but don't want to lose your files, downloaded apps from the Windows Store, and settings, consider using the Refresh procedure. Though less drastic than resetting your computer, a Refresh will often solve your problem.

Refresh Your PC

1. Press Windows logo key+I.
2. Click Change PC Settings.
3. Click General.
4. Scroll down the right pane.
5. Under Refresh Your PC, click the Get Started button.
6. Click Next.
7. Click Refresh.

Tip

When you refresh your computer, it performs the refresh for a few minutes and then restarts. If your problems aren't solved by this procedure, consider following the procedure in Resetting Your PC, earlier in this section.

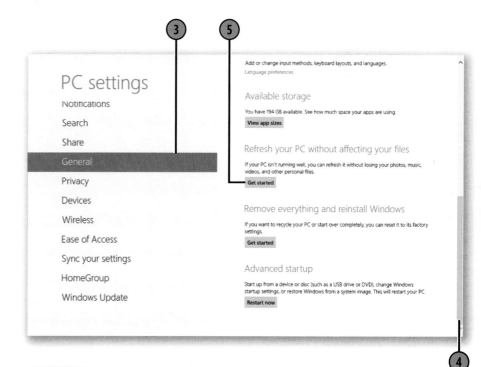

Running Disk Cleanup

When you save data and apps to your hard disk or view or download temporary Internet files, those bits of data can be stored at various locations across your hard disk. Over time, the out-of-date bits of data can cause your computer performance to slow down. Disk Cleanup allows you to erase stray bits of data and consolidate your hard disk to improve your computer's performance.

Run Disk Cleanup

1. On the Start screen, begin to type **Control Panel**.

2. Click the Control Panel app in the results.

3. Click System And Security.

4. Click Free Up Disk Space.

5. Click the drop-down arrow on the Drives field, and select the drives to clean up.

6. Click OK.

7. Clear any check boxes for items that you don't want deleted.

8. Click OK.

9. Click Delete Files.

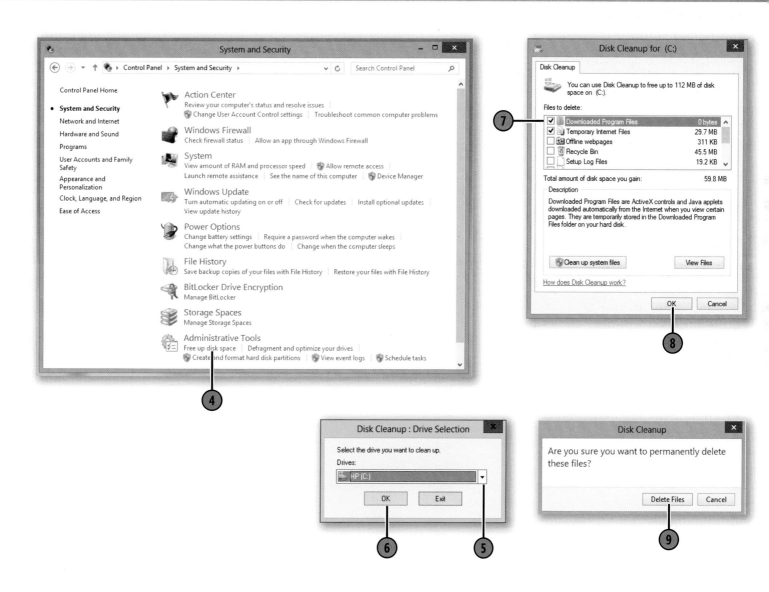

Backing Up Data

Now and then, it's a good idea to back up the files in your computer so that you don't lose anything important. You can use the backup feature in Windows 8 to copy files from libraries, the desktop, your contacts, and your favorites to a specified location, typically an external hard disk. File History is a new backup feature in Windows 8. Essentially, when Windows detects that a change has been made to a file, it will create a new backup of that file. This is a nice safety net, but it doesn't take the place of backing up your files periodically.

Back Up Your Data

1. Connect an external storage device to your computer.

2. On the Start screen, begin to type **Control Panel**.

3. Click the Control Panel app in the results.

4. Click System And Security.

5. Click Save Backup Copies Of Your Files With File History on the next screen.

6. If necessary, click Turn On to turn File History on.

7. When the process is complete, click the Close button.

Defragmenting Your Hard Disk

When Windows saves files, it stores them in non-adjacent areas on your hard disk. A bit of a file can be in one area and other bits in another. Windows uses a directory to tell it where to go on the drive to retrieve all of the bits in the file. Over time, you end up with little fragments of files on your hard disk, including some that don't belong there, perhaps because you deleted a file and a few bits didn't get deleted. Defragmenting your hard drive frees up space by deleting those fragments.

Run the Defragment Utility

1. On the Start screen, begin to type **Control Panel**.

2. Click the Control Panel app in the results.

3. Click System And Security.

4. Click Defragment And Optimize Your Drives.

5. Click to select the drive to clean up.

6. Click Optimize.

7. When the procedure is done, click Close.

Tip

If you'd like to see what the defragment procedure will do before you run it, in step 6, click Analyze instead of Optimize.

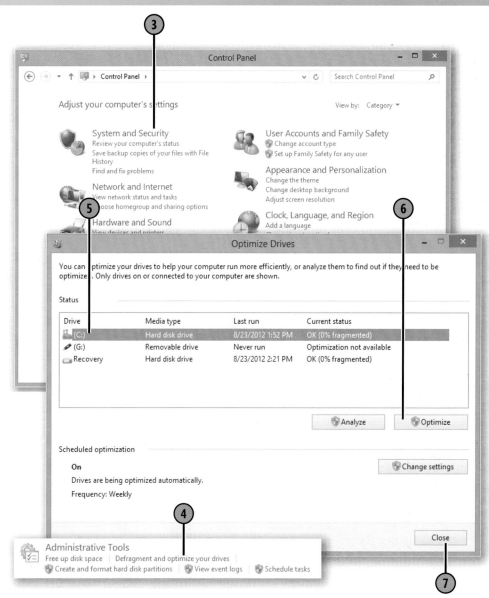

Troubleshooting with Windows Task Manager

Task Manager is a utility program that keeps track of the various programs and processes that are running on your computer. Most of the data in Task Manager will be useful only to very technical people, but Task Manager also enables the rest of us to shut down running programs that might be causing a computer to seize up.

Use Windows Task Manager

1. Press Ctrl+Shift+Esc.

2. Click More Details.

3. Click an active app.

4. Click End Task if you're sure you want to end a task, although you could potentially lose data.

5. Click the Close button.

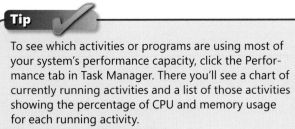

Tip

To see which activities or programs are using most of your system's performance capacity, click the Performance tab in Task Manager. There you'll see a chart of currently running activities and a list of those activities showing the percentage of CPU and memory usage for each running activity.

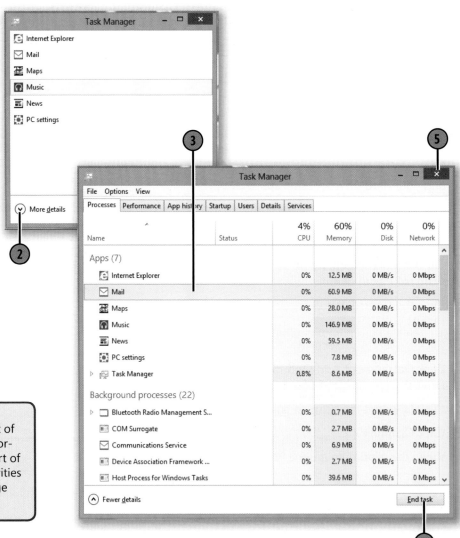

Restarting Your Computer

Sometimes you will need to restart your computer, either because it crashes (stops working) and you want to get it working again or because you've made a change that requires restarting, such as uninstalling a program or downloading updates. Windows 8 provides a Power button in the Settings charm panel so you can quickly perform a restart.

Restart Your Computer

1 Press Windows logo key+I.

2 Click Power.

3 Click Restart.

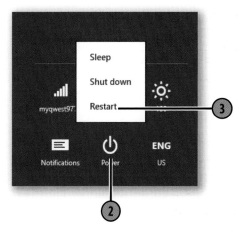

Using Windows Remote Assistance

Remote Assistance involves sending an invitation to somebody asking for help. That person can then click an attachment to the email to accept and access your computer system, move around your computer, and use various tools to pinpoint and fix any problems you might be having. Always make sure that you know and trust any person who you allow to access your computer using Remote Assistance.

Get Remote Help

1. On the Start screen, begin to type **Control Panel**.

2. Click the Control Panel app.

3. Click System And Security.

4. Click Launch Remote Assistance.

5. Click Invite Someone You Trust To Help You.

6. Click Use Email To Send An Invitation to send a message using an email account that you've configured in Windows 8.

7. Enter the recipient's email address.

8. Modify the message if necessary.

9. Click Send.

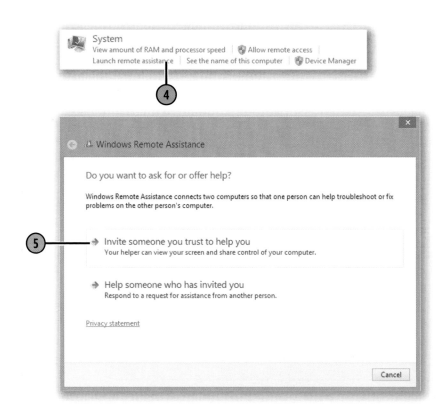

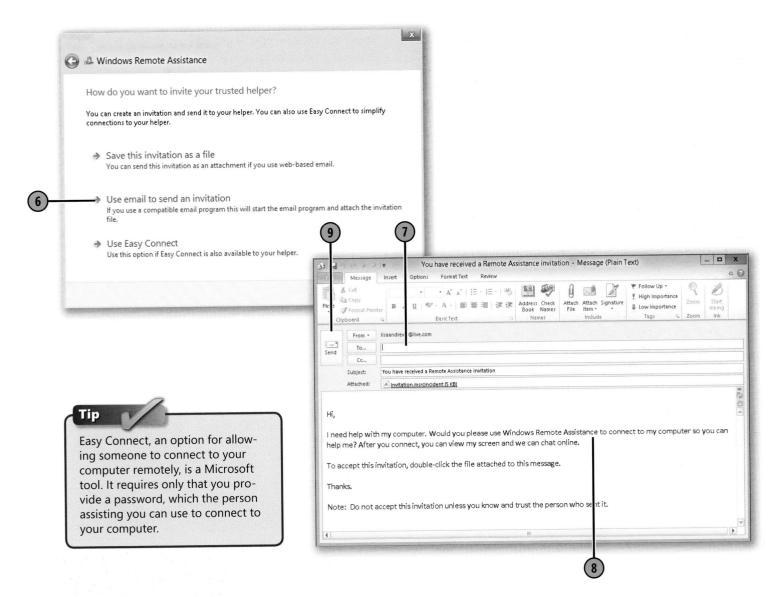

Tip

Easy Connect, an option for allowing someone to connect to your computer remotely, is a Microsoft tool. It requires only that you provide a password, which the person assisting you can use to connect to your computer.

Appendix A
Upgrading to Windows 8

When you move from one version of an operating system to a new one, you need to pay attention to several things. For example, your computer system might need to support certain requirements regarding processor speed and available memory.

Windows 8 comes in six versions, so you need to pick the one that's right for your needs. You also need to be aware of compatibility issues between Windows 8 and software and hardware. The Windows 8 Setup program helps you identify compatibility issues, and Windows Update can help you update hardware drivers, the programs that help hardware interact with Windows.

This appendix also provides a snapshot of what has changed between Windows 7 and Windows 8 so that you know how to find familiar features.

Determining System Requirements

To install Windows 8, your computer has to meet certain system requirements such as the speed of your computer processor or available memory. Check your manufacturer's site for information about your model, or open the Control Panel from your computer, click System And Security, and then click System to view details about it.

Depending on the version of Windows 8 you have, your computer should have a minimum of:

- 1-GHz or faster processor

- 1 GB RAM for 32-bit; 2 GB RAM for 64-bit

- 16 GB available hard disk space for 32-bit; 20 GB for 64-bit

- DirectX 9 graphics device with WDDM 1.0 or higher driver

- Touchscreen if you want to use touch input feature

Understanding Differences Among Windows 8 Versions

There are four versions of Windows 8. Most people will purchase the Home Premium version, which has the most-wanted features, but not necessarily features that business users might want. For them, the Pro version is likely to provide the features they need.

Here's an overview of the various versions of Windows 8:

- Windows 8: the mainstream consumer version of Windows 8. This version has all the features most folks need when using the operating system in a home setting, such as the updated File Explorer, Task Manager, support for switching languages and using multiple monitors.

- Windows 8 Pro: designed for tech enthusiasts and business/technical professionals. Windows 8 Pro adds encryption capability to better protect data, the ability to create virtual machines, PC management tools and domain connectivity. The Windows Media Center is available as an add-on to Windows 8 Pro. Note this is known as the "Media Pack" and is only offered as an add-on to Windows 8 Pro.

- Windows 8 Enterprise: a version that is only available through Microsoft's volume licensing subscription program. Enterprise includes features that are useful to those using Windows 8 in a Windows server environment who require more management tools and security. Enterprise also includes the Windows To Go feature that allows distribution of Windows 8 on USB Pen Drives.

- Windows RT: geared towards portable devices such as tablets, this version doesn't include the management features of Windows 8 Pro or Enterprise.

In addition to choosing one of these editions of Windows, you should select either a 32-bit or 64-bit version.

What's New?

To help you get familiar with where you go to get things done today, The following table lists the key features that have changed from Windows 7 to Windows 8.

Windows 7 vs. Windows 8

Feature	Windows 7	Windows 8
Installation	Up to 20 minutes	Express 8-minute installation
Interface	Desktop	Desktop and Start screen
Input Methods	Mouse, Keyboard	Mouse, Keyboard, Touchscreen
Logon	User name or PIN	User name with Windows Live ID logon supported Picture and PIN

Desktop Shortcut

Taskbar

Start

Jeremy
Nelson

Photos

Desktop

59°
Port Townsend
Cloudy
67°/53°
Weather

Camera

Games

Mus

Internet Explorer

Store   1

People

NJ.com - Ed Lucas Red Sox legend
Johnny Pesky was a class act

Trending
Jennifer Garner
Powerball winner
Little Mermaid surgery

Bing

Mail

Messaging

Maps

SkyDrive

Video

S&P 500
1,418.16 ▲ +0.19% (+2.65)
8/17/2012 4:32 PM EDT

19
Sunday

News

Tiles

Feature	Windows 7	Windows 8
Opening apps	Desktop Start menu	File Explorer or Search charm from desktop or Start screen, respectively or type to search on the Start screen
File Explorer interface	Menus	Graphical ribbon

File Explorer ribbon

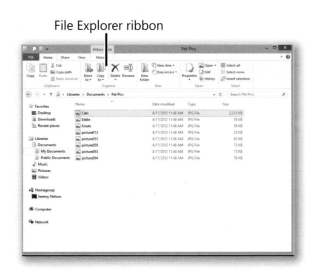

Settings	Control Panel	PC Settings or Control Panel from desktop
Browser	Internet Explorer 9	Internet Explorer 10 desktop and Start screen versions
Searching	Search from Start button	Type on Start screen to search; use Search charm from desktop or Start screen
Live content such as weather	Gadgets	Live tiles on Start screen and Gadgets on desktop
Quick access to apps	Desktop shortcuts	Tiles on Start screen and shortcuts on desktop
Applications	Purchase and install from DVD or online stores	Purchase and install from DVD, Windows Store, or other sources

Using Windows Setup and Program Compatibility Troubleshooter

When using a new version of an operating system, you might experience some transition time as various software and hardware vendors work to update their products to work with the operating system. The Windows 8 Setup program scans your computer to see what's compatible (including apps, devices, and previous versions of Windows on your computer) and generates a Compatibility Summary that you can save or print out to alert you to possible problems. Consider going to a manufacturer's site to look for Windows 8–compatible upgrades that can solve these problems.

You can also choose during the Setup program to keep Windows Settings, Personal Files, and Apps; Just Personal Files; or Nothing. These choices vary based on which version of Windows you upgrade from. In most cases, you should choose the first option to keep all of your apps and files intact.

You can also use the steps that follow to run the Windows Program Compatibility Troubleshooter.

Run the Windows Program Compatibility Troubleshooter

① From the Start screen, type **Control Panel**.

② In the search results, click the Control Panel app.

③ Click Programs.

④ Click Run Programs Made For Previous Versions Of Windows and follow the instructions to test settings.

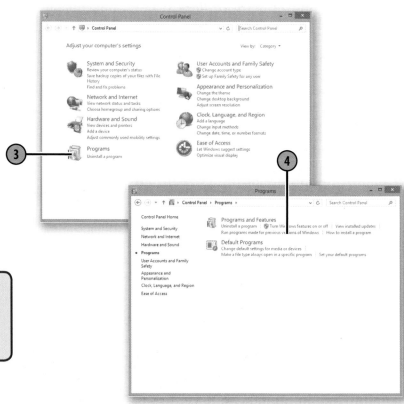

Tip ✓

Be aware of an upgrade issue if you're upgrading from Windows XP. An upgrade will transfer only apps, but no settings or user account files. For this reason, it's a good idea to back up or make note of those system and file settings.

Updating Drivers

Hardware drivers are software programs that help your computer communicate with hardware such as printers, and you can also update hardware drivers automatically by using Windows Update, or manually for each app by using the Windows Device Manager.

See Also

Section 20, "Maintaining and Troubleshooting Your Computer," for the steps to run Windows Update. To update individual drivers, follow these steps.

Update Drivers Manually

① Display the Control Panel.

② Click Hardware And Sound.

③ Click Device Manager.

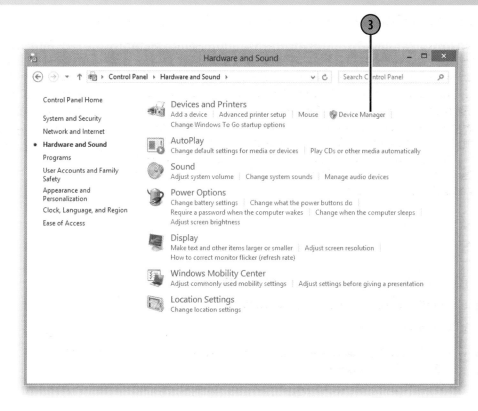

Update Drivers Manually (continued)

④ Right-click a device.

⑤ Choose Properties.

⑥ Click the Driver tab.

⑦ Click the Update Driver button.

⑧ Click Search Automatically For Updated Driver Software.

⑨ If Windows states that your driver is up to date, click Close and then click OK. If Windows reports a newer driver is available, follow the instructions to upgrade.

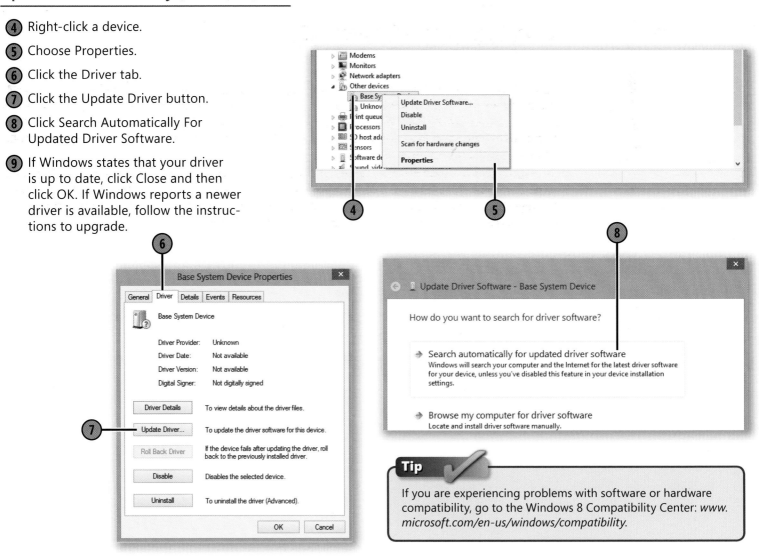

> **Tip**
>
> If you are experiencing problems with software or hardware compatibility, go to the Windows 8 Compatibility Center: *www.microsoft.com/en-us/windows/compatibility*.

Appendix B
Keyboard Shortcuts

Rather than using menus, toolbars, or ribbon buttons to get things done in Windows 8, you can use keyboard shortcuts. A keyboard shortcut is either a function key, such as F1, or a combination of keys, such as Ctrl+C (hold down the first key and without letting go, press the second key), that performs an action such as opening Help or copying selected text. Mastering keyboard shortcuts can make you a more efficient computer user.

Some shortcuts work in the Windows Start screen or desktop or in File Explorer, while others work in software programs such as Microsoft Word or Microsoft Excel. The tables in this chapter list keyboard shortcuts that work with the Windows user interface displayed, and general shortcuts grouped into categories such as Editing and Accessibility.

Windows 8 User Interface Shortcuts

Use This Keystroke Combination	To Do This
Windows logo key+B, D, M, and T	Desktop
Windows logo key+C	Charms
Windows logo key+E	File Explorer
Windows logo key+F	Files
Windows logo key+H	Share
Windows logo key+I	Settings
Windows logo key+K	Devices
Windows logo key+L	Lock screen
Windows logo key+P	Second Screen settings
Windows logo key+Q	Apps
Windows logo key+R	Desktop with Run dialog open
Windows logo key+U	Ease of Access Center
Windows logo key+W	Settings Search
Windows logo key+X	Power User menu displays in lower-left corner
Windows logo key+Z	Toolbar along bottom with All Apps button
Windows logo key+Enter	Launch Narrator

Traditional Windows Shortcuts

Use This Keystroke Combination	To Do This
F1	Display Help for the active app
Ctrl+Esc	Toggle between Windows UI and desktop
Alt+Tab	Switch between open programs
Shift+Delete	Delete item permanently using File Explorer
F10	Activate menu bar options
Ctrl+Shift+Esc	Open Windows Task Manager

Editing Shortcuts

Use This Keystroke Combination	To Do This
Ctrl+C	Copy
Ctrl+X	Cut
Ctrl+V	Paste
Ctrl+B	Bold
Ctrl+U	Underline
Ctrl+I	Italic
Ctrl+Z	Undo last command
Ctrl+A	Select all items in active window

File Explorer Shortcuts

Use This Keystroke Combination	To Do This
F2	Rename selected object
F3	Find all files
Alt+Enter	Open properties for selected object
Press and hold down Ctrl+Shift while dragging a file to the desktop or a folder.	Create a shortcut
F5	Refresh active window.
F6 or Tab	Cycle through panes in File Explorer

Accessibility Shortcuts

Use This Keystroke Combination	To Do This
Press Shift five times	Toggle StickyKeys on and off
Press left mouse button and hold the right Shift key for eight seconds	Toggle FilterKeys on and off
Press down and hold the Num Lock key for five seconds	Toggle ToggleKeys on and off
Left Alt+left Shift+Num+Lock	Toggle MouseKeys on and off
Left Alt+left Shift+Print Screen	Toggle high contrast on and off

Desktop Shortcuts

Use This Keystroke Combination	To Do This
Windows logo key+M	Minimize all
Windows logo key+F1	Help
Shift+Windows logo key+M	Undo minimize all
Windows logo key+Tab	Cycle through open apps
Ctrl+Windows logo key+F	Find computer

Dialog Box Keyboard Commands

Use This Keystroke Combination	To Do This
Tab	Move to the next control in the dialog box.
Shift+Tab	Move to the previous control in the dialog box.
Spacebar	If the current control is a button, this clicks the button. If the current control is a check box, this toggles the check box. If the current control is an option, this selects the option.
Enter	Equivalent to clicking the selected button (the button with the outline).
Esc	Equivalent to clicking the **Cancel** button.
Alt+*underlined letter in dialog box item*	Move to the corresponding item.

Appendix C
Getting Help

Even though Windows 8 provides many intuitive ways to get things done, this new approach can present a learning curve even for those who have used previous versions of Windows. When you run into something in this feature-rich program that you can't figure out, Windows 8 offers a few ways to get help. These resources vary depending on whether you access them from the Start screen or the desktop.

If you go to Help through the Start screen, you see links to a few online articles about working with the Start screen, as well as a link to the Windows website. All the help you access here requires that you have an Internet connection.

When you go to Help from the desktop, you go directly to Windows Help and Support, a database of information that you can use either offline or online. Here you can search for a topic and access articles that walk you through a variety of common Windows tasks.

In addition to the specific help features discussed in this Appendix, be aware that Microsoft will roll out several new help features over the first few months of the Windows 8 launch. For example, Answer Desk is a new service that offers live, premium support 24/7 for customers in the United States, a first for Microsoft. In addition, Windows 8 users get 90 days of free phone support where they can speak with Microsoft Answer Techs. If you find yourself near a Microsoft Store, you can visit the physical Answer Desk located there for help. Should you buy a Signature PC (a PC you buy directly from Microsoft) an Answer Desk app wil be preinstalled on your PC.

Using Start Screen Help

The Start screen is all about being connected, so, logically, the Help features you can access from here require an Internet connection. The benefit to you is that information you find through this method can be updated on a regular basis to give you the most current information about using Windows 8. You can click links to read online articles or visit Microsoft's Windows website.

Read Articles About Using Start Screen

1. With your computer connected to the Internet, from the Start screen, press Windows logo key+I.

2. Click Help.

3. Click one of the three article links.

4. Read the article that appears for help with using Start screen.

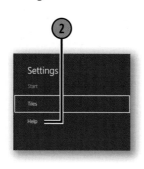

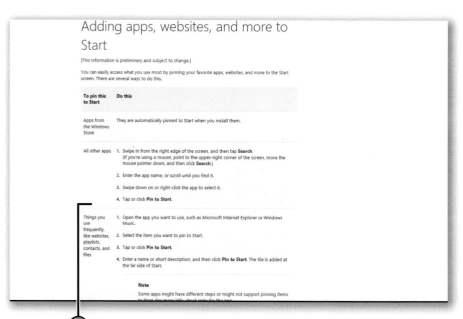

See Also

For information about using Start screen features, see Section 2, "Meet the Windows 8 Interface," to learn about the interface, see Section 3, "Providing Input," to discover the ins and outs of using the touchscreen, and see Section 8, "Searching," for more about searching.

Get Support at the Windows Website

1. With your computer connected to the Internet, from the Start screen, press Windows logo key+I.

2. Click Help.

3. Click Visit The Windows Website.

4. Enter a word or phrase in the Search box.

5. Click Search.

6. Click an article to read it.

7. Click Help and How To.

8. Click a link to get help on a topic.

Tip

Check out the Top Solutions category for the latest advice, and the Downloads menu for additional Windows themes and templates. The Downloads page also includes a Device Drivers section where you can download the latest drivers to keep your hardware peripherals current.

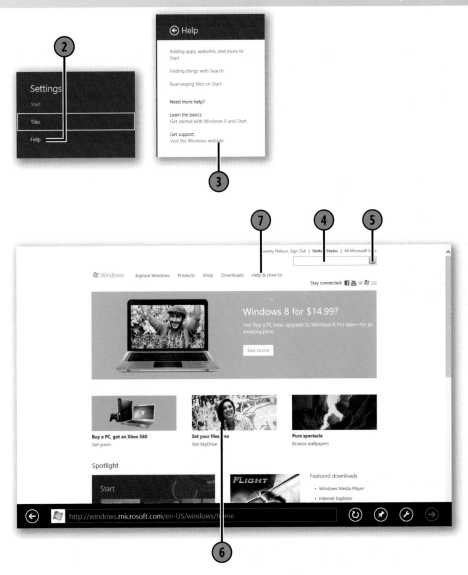

Using Desktop Help

The Help feature (which you can access from the desktop) gives you the option of using offline help or online help. Offline help has the advantage of not requiring an Internet connection. Online help provides the latest help files, which might have been updated more recently than the offline help. After you make the choice about which help to use, you can search by topic or search term for the help you need.

Choose to Use Online or Offline Help

① From the Desktop, press Windows logo key+I.

② Click Help.

③ Click the Offline/Online Help button.

④ Click an option.

Tip

You can use the Zoom feature in the lower-right corner of the Help screen to display help text in a larger or smaller size.

Use Featured Topics

① From the Desktop press Windows logo key+I.

② Click Help.

③ Click a featured topic.

④ Click a subtopic.

⑤ Follow steps.

⑥ Click links to perform actions.

⑦ Follow links to related topics.

⑧ Click to print a topic.

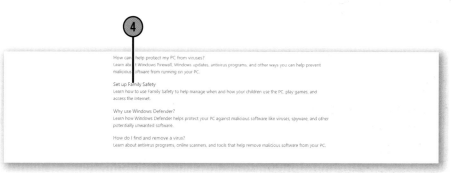

Tip

In some cases, when you click a link to perform an action, it opens a dialog box. In other cases, a wizard opens that walks you through a procedure for applying a setting.

Search for Topics

① With Windows Help And Support displayed from the desktop (see previous task), enter a word or phrase in the Search field.

② Press Enter.

③ Click an item in the search results.

Tip

There are many discussion forums and blogs online that provide help and advice about using Windows, such as Helpwithwindows. com. Search for particular topics by using your web browser. You might find that others have raised similar questions. Finally, you can call Microsoft Technical Support at 1-888-572-5335 and ask about support options.

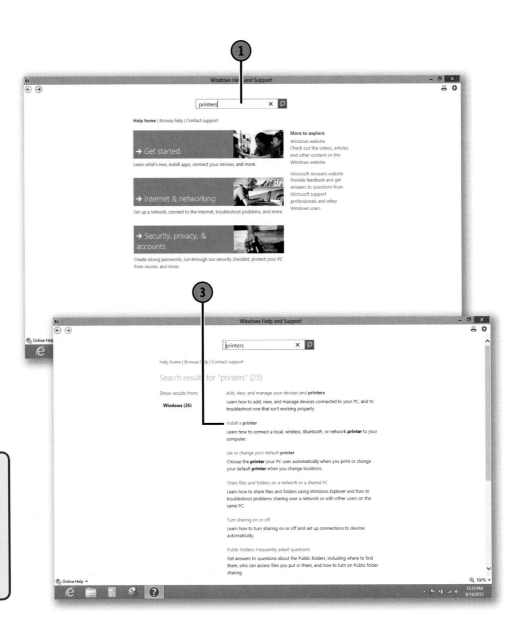

Glossary

A

ACTION CENTER. Indicated by the white flag on the Windows desktop taskbar. This feature aggregates system messages and trouble-shooting help.

ADMINISTRATOR. A user account level at which a user can make changes to an operating system or programs.

APP. A software application, especially those accessed via tiles on the Start screen.

APPLICATION. A software program such as Microsoft Word or Microsoft Internet Explorer.

B

BACKUP. Copies of programs or files kept separate from your computer in case the original file becomes corrupt or is deleted.

BLUETOOTH. A technology that uses radio transmissions to allow interaction between a device, such as printer, mouse, or headset, and your computer or tablet.

BOOKMARK. *See also* Favorites. A list of saved sites to make retrieval of those sites easier.

BOOT. To start a computer when the power is turned off.

BROADBAND. High-speed Internet connections such as Cable or ADSL.

BROWSER. Program used to browse the World Wide Web. For example, Internet Explorer, Firefox, Safari, and Chrome.

BUTTON. A graphical representation of a computer command. When you click or tap a button, the command is executed.

C

CABLE MODEM. A hardware interface required to receive a broadband Internet connection from a cable communications company.

CHARM. A button that provides access to Windows features, such as Start, Search, Sharing, Devices, and Settings.

CD, DVD Disk. Disks provided by software manufacturers to install software on your computer from a CD/DVD drive or used by you to store copies of your files and data.

CHECK BOX. A way to provide on/off input for a feature or setting by selecting or clearing a small box.

CLIP ART. A set of ready-made illustrations and photos you can insert in documents.

CLOUD (The). The practice of hosting programs or services on Internet servers. End users can access these programs or services from their computers without having to install any app locally on their device.

COMPATIBILITY MODE. A special mode in Windows in which programs run in an emulated environment that mimics an earlier version of Windows.

CONTROL PANEL. A set of tools and settings with which you can configure the basic functions of your tablet.

CONTROL KEY. Marked Ctrl on the keyboard. Like Alt and Function keys, this key is used in combination with other keys. Its use can vary from program to program.

CUT or COPY & PASTE. Common tools/menu commands for editing text. With most Windows programs, you can cut or copy a selected item (text or object) and paste it into another place within a document or into another document. Use Ctrl in combination with X, C, and V as shortcuts for cutting, copying, and pasting, respectively.

D

DEFRAGMENT. Reducing the fragmentation (scattering) of files across a hard disk to improve computer performance in retrieving files.

DESKTOP. An alternate interface to the Start screen in which users can control settings and programs in an environment similar to previous versions of Windows.

DEVICE DRIVER. A software program that enables communication between the operating system and a hardware device.

DIALOG BOX. A window that contains sets of commands such as a Font dialog box for formatting text.

DOWNLOAD. The process of transferring files from the web to your computing device. You can download pictures, videos, PDF files, text, and programs.

DRAG-AND-DROP. The facility in most programs to select text or a file and move it to another position or location by using a mouse or finger (on a touchscreen).

DRIVE LETTER. An alphabetical letter from A to Z that Windows assigns to a fixed or removable hard disk.

DVD-ROM. Digital Versatile–Disk Read Only Memory. An optical disk capable of containing much more data than a CD. Used for music, videos, and programs.

DVD-RW. A rewriteable DVD.

DVD Player. A disk player for DVD discs. Capable of playing CDs, as well.

E

E-BOOK. Electronic book.

EMAIL. A service by which you can send messages over the Internet.

EMAIL CLIENT. Program used to send and receive emails such as Windows Live Hotmail or AOL Mail.

F

FAMILY SAFETY. A Windows feature with which you can control children's access to certain features and online content.

FAVORITES. *See also* Bookmarks. A feature of a web browser by which you add frequently used sites to a list for easy retrieval.

FILE EXPLORER. Used to view files, folders, libraries, and networks on the desktop.

FIREWALL. A program that protects your computer from unauthorized access via the Internet.

FLASH DRIVE. A removable storage device that connects to your computer through a USB port.

FONT. A collection of text characters of a pre-defined style, such as Times New Roman or Arial, that can be applied to selected text.

FUNCTION KEYS. Programmable keys F1 to F12 on a keyboard. Function keys vary in their use, depending on the operating system and keyboard.

G

GPS (Global Positioning System). A technology that uses satellites to establish your computer, tablet, or mobile phone's location.

GRAPHICS. The general term used for illustrations, photographs, and other picture objects.

GRAPHICS CARD. The hardware in a computer that controls the monitor or display.

H

HARD COPY. Printed material.

HARD DISK. A disk or set of disks in a computer that is used to record data such as programs and user files.

HARDWARE. Any piece of computing equipment, such as the tablet itself or a printer.

HOMEGROUP. A networking feature through which Windows 8–based computers and devices can share files and printers within a single network.

HOME PAGE. The first page of a website, usually Index.htm. This is the webpage that loads first when you visit a website.

HOTMAIL. A web-based email service run by Microsoft.

HOT SPOT. A Wi-Fi connection in a location such as a café, airport, or hotel over which Wi-Fi enabled laptops, smartphones, or tablets can access the connection.

HYPERLINK. A segment of text or a graphic on a webpage on which you can click or tap that takes you to another webpage. Text links are often colored and underlined; images and maps can also act as links. When using a mouse, the pointer changes shape to that of a hand when hovering over a link. *See* Surfing.

I

IM (Instant Messaging). An app such as Windows Messaging with which you can send text-based messages to people online in real time.

INTEGRATED SEARCH. A feature of Windows with which you can search apps, files, settings, and a variety of web content from the Start screen.

INTERNET. The worldwide network of computer servers that host the data, including the World Wide Web.

INTERNET EXPLORER. The most common web browser, offered for free download or as part of Windows. Other browsers include Mozilla Firefox and Google Chrome.

ISP (Internet Service Provider). A company that provides you with access to the Internet.

L

LOCK SCREEN. The screen that appears when Windows 8 is goes into sleep mode.

M

MALWARE. Malicious software, such as viruses.

MEMORY. Storage capacity in a computer or tablet that Windows uses to store files and run programs.

MONITOR. The computer screen. Also called *display*.

MOTHERBOARD. The main circuit board of a computer, to which components such as computer chips and graphics cards are attached.

MSN. Microsoft Network.

N

NET. A nickname for the Internet.

NETWORK. General term for connected computers.

NOTIFICATIONS. Pop-up notices presented by Windows of important information, such as potential virus threats.

O

OFFLINE. Not connected to the Internet.

ONLINE. Connected to the Internet.

OPERATING SYSTEM. A software interface for a computer in which you can run programs and control devices.

P

PARALLEL PORT. Almost always a 25-pin female socket on the back of a computer which is used for printing but also to attach devices such as scanners and other external equipment. *See also* USB port.

PATH. The location of a file or program on a disk, such as C:\Users\Public, to indicate the Public subfolder in the Users folder located on the C drive.

PC SETTINGS. Common computer or tablet settings that you can access from the Settings charm.

PIN. To place a tile for an app on the Start screen.

PLUG-AND-PLAY. An architecture by which modern computers and hardware (printers, sound cards, DVD players, and so on) are able to recognize when they are connected together, thus enabling easy installation or use.

PORT. Either a physical socket on your computer, such USB, parallel (printer) or Serial communications), or part of the operating system through which communication with your computer takes place (the latter are numbered, for example, Port 110).

PROCESSOR. A physical silicon chip on a motherboard that is the "brain" of a computer or tablet.

Q

QUAD CORE. A processor with four physical cores to more efficiently handle multiple tasks.

R

RAM (Random Access Memory). The temporary storage on a computer. When a computer is shut down, anything stored in RAM is lost.

REFRESH. A way to return a faulty copy of Windows 8 to a properly working copy without losing any files or data.

REGISTRY. A file (one per user on a computer) that contains a database of settings for Windows, user preferences, and installed software and hardware.

REMOTE ASSISTANCE. A feature by which another individual (for example, a Help desk technician) can remotely control a computer over a network or the Internet.

REMOTE DESKTOP. A feature by which you can assume remote control of another computer on a network.

REINSTALL. A way to reset a computer or tablet that is experiencing problems to its original factory settings. All data is lost with this procedure.

S

SAFE MODE. A startup mode that boots Windows in its most basic form, with no background programs in operation. In Safe Mode, the screen displays a very basic (large) layout. Safe Mode is used to troubleshoot and repair various problems in the operating system, including virus removal and defragmentation. To enter Safe Mode, press Shift+F8 upon startup.

SEARCH ENGINE. A program, usually accessed on the Internet, that you use to search for information by entering a few words.

SHAREWARE. Computer programs or software that are free to use, but you are invited to make a contribution toward its development and maintenance costs, typically around $15.

SITE or WEBSITE. An area on the Internet that has its own unique web address (URL). A typical website has a Home page followed by other pages that are linked to the Home page via *hyperlinks*.

SKYDRIVE. Microsoft's online cloud storage solution, found at *http://www.skydrive.com*.

SNAP. A feature that allows you to drag (with a finger or mouse) an open window to the side of the screen to anchor it there.

SOFTWARE. Programs of all kinds which make the computer or tablet act in a particular way to perform certain functions, such as word processing, desktop publishing, and financial calculations.

SPAM. Unsolicited advertising that usually arrives in emails.

SPYWARE. Software that installs itself on your computer without your knowledge which monitors and reports back your activities to its originator.

START SCREEN. The central interface of Windows 8, from which you can access apps and settings.

STREAMING. Receiving sound, video, or pictures over the Internet without having to download the content.

SURFING. Using the hypertext links embedded in a webpage to jump from one website or page to another.

SYSTEM RESTORE. A Windows feature that makes copies of critical system settings and files to be used to restore your system later if required.

T

TAB KEY. Located on the left of the keyboard, you can use this key to jump certain fixed distances across the page when using a word processor, or to jump from one text box to the next when filling out forms, or to move from one table cell to the next when working in a table editor.

TASKBAR. The bar across the bottom of the desktop that contains program and setting icons for quick access.

TEMPORARY FILES. Your Internet browser, some installation programs, and even your own programs can store some files in a part of your hard disk memory. These files are deleted when no longer in use.

TEMPLATE. A standard letter or spreadsheet that forms the basis, or framework, for new documents. Templates can be modified to suit the needs of the current document.

TOOLBAR. An array of icons often found at the top of a program such as a word processor that represent tools and functions you use to carry out tasks.

TOUCHSCREEN. A computer monitor that responds to physical contact by which you provide input to the computer or tablet by touching the screen with a stylus or your finger.

U

UI (USER INTERFACE). A schema to display the user controls for a computer on a monitor. Modern user interfaces are designed to be friendly, intuitive, and usually graphical manner.

UNPIN. To remove a tile from the Windows Start screen.

USER FOLDER. A folder containing a user's files and folders.

URL (Universal Resource Locator). A web address. Web addresses can begin with http:// or www, or both.

USB PORT (Universal Serial Bus). A communication port used to transfer data between your computer and USB devices.

V

VIRUS. A malicious program intended to harm your data or disrupt your computer performance. A virus is spread either from disks or from the Internet.

W

WEB BROWSER. *See* browser.

WI-FI. A wireless interface that uses radio waves to link computers and other devices.

WINDOW. Part of the Windows interface that allows you to view a program, content, or group of settings in a box that you can shrink, enlarge, or display side by side with other windows.

WINDOWS 8. The very latest edition of the Windows operating system on which this book is based.

WINDOWS STORE. An online store containing apps that work with the Windows operating system.

WINDOWS UPDATE. A feature in Windows for automatically updating the operating system with the latest updates and patches.

WIZARD. A program that helps you through a process such as installing new software or hardware.

WPA. An encryption method for wireless networks.

WWW (World Wide Web). Documents stored on the Internet.

Z

ZIP FILE. A file in which data is compressed to take up less space. Files in zip or compressed files must be extracted to be used.

Index

Symbols

" " (quotation marks) for searching, 166

A

accessibility settings. *See* Ease Of Access
    panel
accounts
    Account Control Settings, 61
    Account Settings button (Start screen),
        12
    online, 198–199
AccuWeather website, 210
Add a Bluetooth Device setting, 255
Add a Device process, 252–253
Add A New Credit Card option
    (Marketplace), 242
address bar (Internet Explorer), 34, 164
addresses, in Maps app, 196
Add Tab button (Internet Explorer 10), 168
administrative privileges, 80
Advanced Printer Setup, 253
Advanced Startup, 268
Aerial View (Maps), 215
Album option (Windows Media Player),
    248
All Apps button (Start screen), 34, 114
All Categories option (Windows Store),
    186
All Contacts screen (People app), 200
All Genres list (music), 238

Allow And Block List setting (Family
    Safety), 86
Allow Bluetooth Devices To Find This
    Computer setting, 254
Allow Or Block Games And Windows Store
    Apps By Rating link, 90
All Prices option (Windows Store), 186
Always Notify level (account control), 82
Analyze instead of Optimize setting
    (defragmenting), 273
apps
    accessing with shortcuts (Desktop), 18
    allowing to access computers, 64–67
    app tiles, setting photos as, 223
    buying, 191
    categories in Windows Store, 187
    closing, 26, 126
    displaying recently used, 26, 36
    entering/formatting text in, 118–119
    inserting objects, 121
    opening in windows on Desktop, 16
    opening with tiles, 13
    overview, 113
    printing documents from, 122
    rating/reviewing, 192
    reading reviews of, 188
    saving files, 123
    searching for, 110, 186
    setting which to search for, 112
    snapping windows in, 30
    Spotlight category, 187
    uninstalling, 127
    unpinning from Start screen, 189
    using menus, 115
    using ribbons (WordPad), 116–117
    using toolbars, 116–117

viewing purchased/installed, 190
Windows clipboard, 120
Xbox, 124–125
Arial font, 119
Artist category (Windows Media Player),
    248
attachments (email)
    adding to messages, 180
    opening/reading, 178
    paperclip icon indicator, 173

B

back-facing camera, 230
background, Desktop, 15
backing up files, 148–149, 272
Bing Maps, 196
Bing search engine (Internet Explorer 10),
    167
Birthday calendar, 202
blind carbon copies (email), 179
Block All Incoming Connections check
    box, 62
Bluetooth devices, connecting to, 254–255
Bold button (WordPad), 118
booting computers from disc, 268
brightness settings (Camera app), 231
Browse By Date button (Pictures library),
    224
Burn tab (Windows Media Player), 248
Burn to Disc button (File Explorer Share
    tab), 149
buying
    Buy Points button (Microsoft), 226
    points (Music app), 242–243
    videos, 226–227

C

Calendar app
    adding events, 203
    deleting events, 207
    displaying views, 202
    editing existing events, 206
    inviting people to events, 205
    reminders, 204
Camera app
    Camera Options dialog box, 231
    changing cameras and modes, 230
    setting camera resolution, 231
caret browsing
    defined, 93
    setting, 101
cell phones, tethering computers to, 259
Celsius temperature (Weather app), 208
Change PC Settings button, 66
charms
    basics, 14
    displaying/using from Start screen, 12
    displaying with mouse, 26
    search menu, 137
    techniques for displaying, 32
Clear List button (playlists), 250
Clear Map button, 219
clip art, 121
Clipboard, Windows, 120
closing
    apps, 26, 126
    Close key (touch keyboards), 31
    windows, 16
collating copies (printing), 122
Collections, music (Music app), 244
compressed files
    adding files to, 147
    creating, 146
computers. *See* PCs (Personal Computers)

Confirming PCs for syncing, 154–155
connecting
    to Bluetooth devices, 254–255
    Connect Automatically check box
        (networks), 257
    to networks, 257
    printers to computers, 252–253
contacts (People app)
    adding, 194–195
    editing information, 196–197
    pinning to Start screen, 201
    sending messages to, 198
content-specific tabs (File Explorer), 131
contrast, changing (screens), 100
contrast settings (Camera app), 231
Control Panel app, 10, 62
copying
    files to folders, 145
    text/objects to Windows Clipboard
        (WordPad), 120
copyrighted websites, 165
countdown timer for photos/videos, 232
CPU/memory usage for running activities,
    274
credit cards, 242–244
Cursor Thickness list (mouse), 97
customizing
    Custom Scan option (Windows
        Defender), 69
    searches, 111
    Windows Firewall Customize Settings
        dialog box (Windows Firewall), 62

D

data, backing up, 272
DataEraser software, 151
Date and Time button (WordPad ribbon),
    116–117
defragmenting hard drives, 273

deleting
    Delete button (video playback), 233
    events (Calendar app), 207
    files/folders, 150–151
    files from SkyDrive, 161
    files with disk cleanup, 270
    Frequent sites, 169
    IM threads, 183
    search history, 111
    shortcuts, 18
Desktop
    accessing Help from, 296–298
    accessing Internet Explorer from, 10
    adding shortcuts to, 18
    apps, opening, 114
    displaying charms from, 32
    displaying Internet Explorer 10 from,
        170
    keyboard shortcuts, 290
    overview, 15
    switching between Start screen and,
        10–11
    taskbar basics, 19
Details page (Calendar app), 207
Details Pane button (File Explorer View
    tab), 138
Details View button (SkyDrive), 160
Device Drivers section (Windows 8), 295
Devices And Printers (Control Panel), 94
dialog box keyboard shortcuts, 291
dialog launcher symbol, 117
directions for travelling (Maps), 219
Disk Cleanup, 270–271
displaying
    Calendar app views, 202
    charms, 32
    Display Pointer Trails checkbox, 97
    subfolders (File Explorer), 136
    tools via right-clicking, 34–35
    touch keyboard, 31

X

Xbox
  apps, 124–125
  option to play back videos on, 229

Z

zipped folders, 146
zooming
  Maps, 214
    Zoom In button (WordPad ribbon),
      116–117
Zune online store, 242

About the Author

Nancy Muir is the author of more than 100 books on technology topics, ranging from Microsoft Windows and Microsoft Office to nanotechnology and Internet safety. She runs a website, TechSmartSenior.com, that provides information about computers and the Internet for seniors, as well as writing a column on computers for Retirenet.com. Prior to her writing career, Nancy worked in computer book publishing as a software training manager at Symantec Corporation. She holds a certificate in distance learning design from the University of Washington, and has taught technical writing and online safety at the university level.

What do you think of this book?

We want to hear from you!

To participate in a brief online survey, please visit:

microsoft.com/learning/booksurvey

Tell us how well this book meets your needs—what works effectively, and what we can do better.
Your feedback will help us continually improve our books and learning resources for you.

Thank you in advance for your input!